Helping Children to Manage Loss

of related interest

Talking with Children and Young People about Death and Dying
A Workbook
Mary Turner, illustrated by Bob Thomas
ISBN 185302 563 1 A4 pb

Interventions with Bereaved Children
Edited by Susan C Smith and Margaret Pennells
ISBN 185302 285 3 pb

Group Work with Children and Adolescents
A Handbook
Edited by Kedar Nath Dwivedi
ISBN 185302 157 1 pb

Children and Divorce
Chain Reaction
Ofra Ayalon and Adina Flasher
ISBN 185302 136 9 pb

The Grief Game
Yvonne Searle and Isabelle Streng
ISBN 185302 333 7

The Divorced and Separated Game
Yvonne Searle and Isabelle Streng
ISBN 185302 334 5

The Forgotten Mourners
Guidelines for Working with Bereaved Children
Sister Margaret Pennells and Susan C Smith
ISBN 1 85302 264 0 pb

Grief in Children
A Handbook for Adults
Atle Dyregrov
ISBN 1 85302 113 X pb

Helping Children to Manage Loss

Positive Strategies for Renewal and Growth

Brenda Mallon

Jessica Kingsley Publishers
London and Philadelphia

Acknowledgements:

My heartfelt thanks to the children, parents, teachers and clients who spoke so eloquently of their experience of loss – I hope I have told your stories with the same truth as that with which they were revealed. And to so many friends and strangers who cared enough for others to tell of their hurts, to share their feelings about growth through pain – I hope I have expressed your views accurately. Without such honesty about painful times this book could not have been written, and I am indebted to all who so willingly shared their dark nights of the soul as well as their glorious renewals.

Brenda Mallon, August 1997, Manchester

Extract from *I'm Still Running* (1988) by Tracy Wollington reproduced with kind permission of her parents. Extract from *Boy* (1986) by Roald Dahl reproduced with kind permission of David Higham Associates Ltd. Poems from the *Cadbury's Book of Children's Poetry* reproduced with kind permission of Cadbury Schweppes Ltd. Every effort has been made to contact copyright holders for their permission to reproduce material in this book. The publishers would be grateful to hear from any copyright holder who is not here acknowledged, and undertake to rectify any errors or omissions in future editions of this volume.

First published in the United Kingdom in 1998 by
Jessica Kingsley Publishers Ltd
116 Pentonville Road
London N1 9JB, England
and
325 Chestnut Street
Philadelphia, PA 19106,
USA

Copyright © 1998 Brenda Mallon

Library of Congress Cataloging in Publication Data
A CIP catalogue record for this book is available from the Library of Congress

British Library Cataloguing in Publication Data
A CIP catalogue record for this book is available from the British Library

Printed and Bound in Great Britain by
Athenaeum Press, Gateshead, Tyne & Wear

Contents

Children Learn What They Live

If
a child lives with criticism,
she learns to condemn

If
a child lives with hostility,
he learns to fight.

If
a child lives with ridicule,
she learns to be shy.

If
a child lives with shame,
he learns to feel guilt.

If
a child lives with tolerance,
she learns to be patient.

If
a child lives with praise,
he learns to appreciate.

If
a child lives with encouragement,
she learns confidence.

If
a child lives with fairness,
he learns justice.

If
a child lives with security,
she learns to have faith.

If
a child lives with approval,
he learns to like himself.

If
a child lives with acceptance and friendship,
he or she learns to find love in the world.

INTRODUCTION

I knew I was different from other children because there were no kisses or promises in my life. I often felt lonely and wanted to die. I would try to cheer myself up with daydreams. I never dreamed of anyone loving me as I saw other children loved. That was too a big a stretch for my imagination. I compromised by dreaming of my attracting someone's attention...of having people look at me and say my name. (Marilyn Monroe 1975)

Only the confirmed sentimentalist still believes childhood is a time of untroubled innocence. The reality is that thousands of children every week suffer loss and, like Marilyn Monroe quoted above, feel troubled and unloved. Over 10,000 young people between the ages of ten and eighteen lose a parent each year through death, others suffer the despair and disruption of separation or divorce.

Children's distress reflects the world we adults have made for them. Rising numbers of children on 'at risk' registers, 98,000 children running away from home each year, increased rates of teenage suicide, depression and anorexia, and in excess of 10,000 calls a day to ChildLine show us just how widespread is the strain. Our children, be they in cities or in rural communities, are confronted in their formative years with all sorts of traumatic events: illness, disability, divorce, bereavement, bullying, failure and natural disasters. They see, as do adults, the television news of the almost incomprehensible horror of a tragedy such as occurred in Dunblane, or the misery of Bosnia.

In my work as a counsellor I have learnt much about both the short term and long term effects of stress in children's lives. The potential for stress is implicit too in certain transitional stages of development, for instance at adolescence when the individual must adjust to the physiological, psychological and social changes of growing up. Working with teachers I have devised strategies to ease some of the distress that inevitably floods over into school life, be it in the form of sadness or aggression. Perhaps most importantly I have listened to what children say they want adults to do at such times. Their personal accounts give touching insights to a world we all too often overlook.

This book came about in response to requests from parents and teachers who, when faced with very distressed children, did not know what to do for the best. Many felt a complete lack of confidence in their own ability to help, having been undermined in the past by those who claimed to know to the 'best' – or 'only' – way to respond to children. However, this approach denies the crucial truth that reliable love and commitment are the most important factors in enabling a child to come to terms with loss. Each of us *can* help children face their difficulties, and anyone who has a role in caring for children, be they teachers, doctors, psychologists or nursing staff, can do much to empower children and their families to face the impact of loss.

The book is also written as a response to those many children who have told me very clearly what they do – and do not – want when they face a stressful situation, for example when their parents split up, when they are bereaved or when they suffer major illness. Of course all change is stressful to some degree, but in this book I am concerned with a level of stress that is likely to cause distress. That is when the child feels overwhelmed by the situation, unable to make sense of it, and begins to suffer in particular ways which, if left unrecognised, could cause long term damage.

Grief is one of the great unacknowledged hurts that our children face. Most adults cannot cope with their own grief, let alone a child's, and too often we deny the impact of loss, saying 'Oh look, Jenny's playing. See, she's over it now. It didn't really affect her.' But loss quite definitely does affect children, as you will see from those whose words are recorded here.

When considering the effects of stress on children we need to remember that it is often intensified because they have no power over those who directly control their lives. When a marriage breaks up the child usually has no power to influence the changes set in train – the move to a different house or the loss of one parent from their usual home, the change of school if they relocate, the loss of friends, the teasing of peers, the different status. It may be a situation they would never have chosen but the child has to cope. We have a responsibility to help heal the inflicted pain and to recognise the ways children communicate their distress.

The severe strain felt by parents often ripples through the family, and caught up as they are, in the maelstrom of their own emotions, parents find it hard to simultaneously deal with the increased demands of disrupted children and their own loss. Others who have regular contact with the child – counsellors, teachers – may find more demands on their time and patience. There are many strategies to alleviate the pain of these children who are facing or have faced loss. The voices of real children, real men and real women who share their stories of pain and renewal, tell us what helped them to survive their losses and how they came to be strengthened by their experiences. All names have been changed to maintain confidentiality.

Brenda Mallon

CHAPTER 1

Setting the Scene
The Loss of Childhood

When adults think about 'loss', we usually think of critical life events such as death or divorce, yet when children are asked about loss their range of associations is sometimes startling. Children talk of the hurt of losing their best friend because of an argument, of looking foolish in front of their peers, of ceasing to have a parent's attention after the birth of a younger sibling, or of feeling bereft when the school gerbil dies. In our adult 'superiority' we frequently dismiss or trivialise these events as minor tribulations. Our body language conveys the message, 'Oh, that isn't real loss, I know about "real" loss!', as if we have insider knowledge of a league table of loss that a child cannot know! But loss is loss. What children feel is the real truth, and this is what we need to keep to the forefront of our minds in any work with children.

The pain of loss in childhood is a raw, penetrating hurt that can be devastating. Adults have the benefit of past knowledge and experience to put loss into perspective, for children this is not the case. Whilst we may have found ways of coming to terms with sorrow – found coping strategies, seen how others managed or believe that the pain will pass as it has in the past – children do not have that comforting knowledge, however meagre it may be. Too often we 'mature' ones have become de-sensitised to early suffering and ignore the profound emotions that loss in childhood provokes. The words of the children in the chapters that follow will take you into their reality – they describe the strain of loss in their lives and renewal thereafter.

Without a shadow of doubt children experience loss. Even babies in their first year who are affected by loss in the family are aware that something is wrong, something has changed, though they may not be 'told'. As they pine and look out for a loved one who has gone away for example, their distress is self evident. They pick up signs from those closest to them that something is amiss, and it shows. Sometimes words are not possible because the child has not yet learned to speak, yet that does not mean they do not feel the pain (Bowlby 1990).

When Toby's father was posted overseas the family moved closer to the maternal grandmother. This involved relocation to a new house, a new play group and losing regular contact with his paternal grandparents who had lived just around the corner. Toby at three years old went through all sorts of grieving, and after twelve months when his father returned he refused to acknowledge the stranger. He would not be picked up by him and in reserved shyness clung to his mother. His parents were surprised yet Toby's reaction is perfectly in line with what usually happens when babies are left by someone they love. Protest, in the form of angry tears and rage, is followed by despair, sadness and giving up hope, which if the loved one does not return, climaxes in detachment. His father's absence caused Toby to detach and later re-unification with the 'stranger' was not simple.

Any child may experience bereavement, separation, divorce or a life threatening illness. Some children live in the midst of civil conflict or war or survive disaster. Others suffer the strain of abuse, failure or rejection. Yet more know the misery of bullying, of being labelled a 'no-hoper' or just being ignored by a seemingly uncaring world. These losses all affect the child and influence the adult person they will become. Too often the child has no one to turn to, no one to guide them through these experiences, and frequently professional help in the form of counselling or psychotherapeutic support is neither offered nor seen as pertinent. Yet, as there are well recognised ways of travelling that path from despair to emotional wellbeing, there is no reason for a child to suffer more through ignorance.

If we can recognise the strain and accept the validity of the child's voice then we can do something to ease the pain. Children do express their distress if relatives, family, friends and teachers give time to listen, or where words fail they communicate through their body language and in acting out behaviour. This is something we will return to in later chapters. Also, peers of a distressed child will sometimes alert adults and seek help on their behalf. If you remain open to the variety of ways that children communicate you can offer appropriate support at the earliest point of intervention.

Coming to terms with death is one of the most important lessons a child has to learn about life. Preparing for death usually happens long before a person has to face the death of a loved one. It starts with learning that flowers bloom then fade and die; seeing moths circle the light that burns them, and knowing pets that die. If we talk about events and help children manage these 'smaller deaths' they will be more able to manage the strain and pain if they are ever faced with the loss of someone they love. You will find that Chapter 2, 'Preparing For Loss' concentrates on this aspect of children's response to death.

The death of a significant person in our lives is probably the most difficult, painful task we will have to face in life. Every day in Britain 40 children lose a parent, 550 women lose their husbands and 140 men lose their wives, and thousands of other close relationships end. Yet despite these figures we are still tongue-tied and embarrassed when faced with the strong emotions such loss arouses.

As children grow up they see inhibited responses and learn without being told that some subjects are taboo. Often, where adults seek professional help through specialist counselling agencies such as Relate or Cruise, children are not informed. For many there is still a stigma attached to counselling and therapy, so parents hide their own needs and vulnerabilities. To get over this crippling uneasiness adults need to be more open about loss and let sorrow find words. If we are more willing to admit our own feelings then it is easier for children to voice theirs. When counselling such children, limited, appropriate disclosure about our own experiences of loss may facilitate the expression of the child's emotions.

We need more openness too about another ending: that is, the 'death' of a marriage. Divorce, one of the most serious crises of our age, produces victims and survivors. There is no such thing as a victimless divorce. Even where there are no children involved there is disappointment for the couple — disappointment that early expectations were not fulfilled, that their partner was not the person hoped for, regret that one or both changed and developed different life paths. Where children are involved the casualty rate soars and the scars of divorce may remain for a lifetime, which is why children's reactions need to be considered as soon as parents realise their marriage may end.

There is no sugar-coating for the bitter effects of divorce, and professionals need to recognise this no matter what their personal views are on the subject. No matter how liberal we may be, the reality is that divorce hurts children – the facts are unpalatable and often denied. But just how badly are children affected?

Vast numbers of children are deserted after divorce. One in five children can expect their parents to divorce before they are sixteen and about half of these children will lose contact with their father within two years. The daunting truth is that one in three marriages end in divorce, giving Britain the highest divorce rate in Europe. Women lose an average of half their income after divorce, which means their children grow up in poorer housing and in significantly worse material circumstances than children in the same social class whose parents did not divorce. Eleven-year-old Kevin is far from unusual:

When my Mum and Dad got divorced I didn't like it one bit. I don't like how my Dad has got engaged to someone else and I still haven't got over it fully although they've been divorced for six years. When I moved I didn't like it but there was nothing that could help me having to live in this dump.

Voices such as Kevin's often go unheard.

Sally has had many losses in her nine years. Because of a rapidly deteriorating marriage, her mother took Sally and her brother to a refuge run by the local council. They had to leave home in a rush and so they did not even have a change of clothes. The next day Sally went to school in ill-fitting, well-worn clothes that were obviously not her own. Sally's teacher described how her pupil was extremely disturbed and upset not just about the loss of her home in this instance, but her loss of privacy, loss of stability and the loss of basic possessions such as her clothes and toys. The objects that had made her life stable were all gone, apart from her brother and mother that is, but they too were in a state of confused distress. Sally's story of loss is only one small example of the strain children may undergo, there are many similar and many more harrowing.

Coming to terms with broken dreams and broken promises takes a long time for adults as well as children. But in considering the effects of loss and resultant stress we need to recognise that individual responses vary. A proportion of children appear to come through relatively unscathed whilst others experiencing outwardly similar situations become severely disturbed. Evidence shows that such change is most damaging to those who are already genetically vulnerable to psychiatric disorder. These internal pressures are in turn affected by external events so, apart from the loss of security that Sally experienced, further factors begin to impinge, in her case other people's reactions. Although the social stigma of divorce is not as stinging now as it once was, signs of a backlash against certain single-parent families erupt intermittently.

The psychological aftermath of divorce and separation has grave implications for adults as well as children. We now know that it is common for both divorced partners to suffer severe depression for a couple of years after their separation. Divorced people are twenty four times more likely to commit suicide, seven times more likely to die of cirrhosis of the liver due to alcohol abuse and four times more likely to die in a car crash. It is a bleak picture and it does not stop there.

There is overwhelming, incontrovertible evidence to show that children are damaged by divorce. In families where one of the parents does not take a personal, active, long-term responsibility for their children, those children are disadvantaged in just about every aspect of their lives, whatever their social class or economic circumstances (Halsey and Dennis 1991). No matter how good the new situation turns out to be all divorce involves pain. It leaves many children with an irretrievable sense of loss of their childhood. Mavis MacClean (MacClean and Wadsworth 1988) of Oxford University has been charting the progress of a group of children born in the same week in March 1946 and her findings, like those of American investigations into the effects of divorce, give no room for complacency.

The research results show that long term girls do worse than boys. Initially, straight after the divorce, boys are more aggressive, disruptive and likely to be in trouble at school, and are more prone to bedwetting. Both boys and girls equally suffer nightmares, nail biting and speech problems, but then boys seem to pick up the pieces and move on. Girls on the other hand appear to cope much better initially, as if they take the divorce in their stride. However, MacClean's research sample showed that as children of divorced parents reached their twenties, especially girls, 'the Sleeper Effect', a term coined by Wallerstein and Blakeslee (1990), wears off. Pent up anger and disappointment, so well concealed by girls for years, emerged in the form of depression. All too often anger repressed and turned inwards causes depression.

The young women, as they had become, failed to form long lasting nurturing partnerships, instead they were more likely to be involved in abusive relationships. They were more likely to suffer psychiatric difficulties and have drink related problems, while a high percentage of the men in the study were in low paid jobs or unemployed, and were much more prone to be involved in delinquent behaviour by the age of twenty one, especially if the parents had divorced before their child was five years old.

Dr Judith Wallerstein, one of the world's foremost experts on divorce and its effects, runs The Centre For The Family In Transition. She and her team have been responsible for counselling more divorcing families than any other American agency, and have found that whilst divorce for adults is the closing of one chapter and the opening of a new one, for children it is quite a different matter. A child has no sense of a break. Also children internalise the image of the first family, and that image, often idealised, remains a permanent part of their perception of relationships. All too many children find divorce represents the end of childhood (see Wallerstein and Blakeslee 1990).

For Adam such idealisation caused enormous stress. Aged seven when his parents divorced, Adam was severely distressed for many years. He attended a youth club for under-eleven's and one day when he arrived he said he had been attacked by a man. The police were called and Barbara, one of the specialist counselling workers at the centre, talked to him whilst they waited for his mother to arrive. Barbara recognised his evident distress yet somehow the details of the assault just did not tally; the injury to his face did not match the description Adam gave as to how he sustained it. Finally Barbara, sensing deeper levels of hurt, said that as the police were involved his estranged father would probably need to be told too. At that point Adam broke down and admitted he had made the whole thing up.

It emerged that Adam desperately wanted to see his father and believed contact would be renewed if he got hurt in a dramatic way. Surely, he reasoned, his father would come if there was an attack? Coupled with that hope was ambivalence because Adam also knew that his father's violent temper might erupt and end in a beating for telling lies. The boy was trapped between an aching desire to see his father and a desperate fear of the consequences if he was caught lying. The boy explained to Barbara that he had fallen against a brick wall accidentally. He felt so upset and hurt in that split second that he needed to see his Dad more than anyone else in the world, and without really thinking he concocted the story in the hope he would get the attention he so craved.

There was a similar feeling when twelve-year-old Tom talked about his life:

I've had many losses in my life… My parents have split up and my Gran and Grandad have split up. I can't keep in touch with my Dad. I hate him for what he did to my Mum by having an affair. I don't forgive him for what he did but I would go to London, that's where we used to live, and visit him. If ever I have the chance I will go to London and visit him.

Tom's ambivalence is plain. At one and the same time he 'hates' his father yet longs to see him again. He champions his mother, offers explicit support by remaining unforgiving, yet fantasises about the chance to visit his missing father. The tragedy is doubled for Tom because not only have his parents separated but his grandparents too. What has Tom learned about the stability of relationships from his life experiences in his twelve years to date?

Though the effects of divorce can be devastating, thankfully not all children are affected in the same way or to the same degree. Studies show that about one third do not appear to suffer any significant long term affects. The ones who managed best had parents who handled the divorce carefully and sensitively, did not fight over the children, kept up regular contact subsequently and maintained close emotional bonds. This is something we will return to later in 'Strategies For Renewal', Chapter 9.

The breakdown of their parents' marriage may in fact be good news for some children. For them living in a conflict-ridden family can be more damaging than living in a stable home with one parent; in this case divorce is a positive way of escaping a destructive family life. Whatever their reasons, some of which we will hear later, these children feel much happier and very often safer living with one parent they trust. They do not want their parents to get back together and sometimes fear that the absent parent may come back and snatch them away. Such anxieties often remain unmentioned, but where you can recognise that the child is feeling vulnerable special efforts need to be made to reassure and protect them.

In any scene-setting about loss in childhood, it soon becomes apparent that we are not talking about one moment in a child's life or one event, however traumatic that may be. Instead, what we know is that the single loss often sets off a train of other reactions in the child's life, as it does in those lines of dominoes where when the first falls it sets off a chain reaction, until all the dominoes in the series are affected. We can follow this through in Linda's story, because it encapsulates so many of the issues triggered by one event, in this case a tragic death.

Linda's husband Ian, a computer program manager, thirty-nine years old and enjoying excellent health, left on Friday morning to work away as he often did. He rang on Saturday night from his hotel room, to say he was just on his way to have dinner with some colleagues. Before their conversation ended however there was a silence for a couple of minutes, which was broken when Ian said he must have fallen off the bed or blacked out for a minute. He put it down to tiredness and said he would not have a drink and would try to get an early night.

At eleven o'clock a Dr Duprais rang Linda to say her husband was in hospital. Ian had taken ill at the restaurant and he kept losing consciousness. At half-hourly intervals Linda rang the hospital 300 miles away on the other side of England, whilst upstairs her children aged three and five slept. At two thirty in the morning they were being cared for by a relative as she drove through the night, her head hammering with the news that Ian had had a stroke and that she should go to the hospital immediately. The news was bad. She said, 'It was just no good. He was on a respirator but he never regained consciousness.' After hours of tests he was declared brain dead.

Alone in the hospital far from her family and friends, Linda reacted by becoming 'organised', telling the hospital staff that her husband was a kidney donor and wished his organs to be used to help others, and by quickly taking action:

> I was in shock but I had to get back to Manchester. Mum and Dad were there looking after the children. I felt I couldn't speak to them on the phone but I arranged for them to go to my sister. When I got back to Janice's I put

on a front. I told them that he wasn't well and in hospital. The children accepted that. On the Tuesday I wanted them to go to school and I still did not tell them what had happened. My neighbour took them to school and told the Headmaster what had happened. On Tuesday afternoon after tea, my brother and I told the children. I told them he had been very poorly and he would not be coming home again. Five year old Thomas immediately started crying. Three year old Helen did not really register what was going on but she cried because everyone else was crying. We all had cuddle and Thomas asked 'Won't I ever see him?' and I said, 'Well, he's in heaven now.' They seemed OK really. I gave a photo of Ian to each of them and they kept it by their bed and they used to kiss that photograph goodnight. It is three years now and that really broke my heart. The children would sometimes say 'I miss you Dad.' And Helen used to cry and say 'I wish I could fly to the sky and bring Daddy down'.

Linda's decision to delay telling her children until she got home meant that she could be there when they got the news. She felt that she had to be the one to tell them, and knew that if she too was missing when they found out their father was dead, they would have been thrown into a state of panic, believing that she too had gone forever. It was crucial that they be together at the critical moment of disclosure, and the additional presence of her brother reassured Linda that there was someone else they loved and trusted who could help out if she became distraught.

Linda did not tell the children about the funeral, they were sent to school as usual. At the time she felt they were too young, though with the benefit of hindsight she wonders if it was the best decision. Once, later, when Linda passed a gravestone with Thomas he asked, 'Has my Dad got one of those?' When I said 'No', he said 'Well, what has he got?' She explained that Ian had wanted to be buried but did not want a headstone. Instead, Linda had a bench with a special verse inscribed on a brass plaque put the local golf course.

Thomas seemed relieved that there was something tangible to mark his father's death, and it meant a great deal to him that a trophy was given to his school in memory of his father. Such rituals mark life events and, as Thomas knew intuitively, they help in the healing process and form a link between past and future, making the present more bearable.

Linda showed me a picture that Thomas had drawn two weeks after Ian's death. It was divided equally into an upper and lower half. In the bottom half was their house, smoke curling out of the chimney with Thomas and Linda in the garden and the blue sky above the house. In the upper half of the picture, in the centre, Thomas drew his father in the garden of a smaller house, complete with TV aerial and for all the world the same as his earthly home. The children found comfort in the 'mirror world' as Linda calls it, 'I used to say to the children 'What do you think Daddy is doing?' We used to laugh and say he'd probably be playing golf!'

Sometime later though, a neighbour died and Thomas cried and said, 'Oh no, not another one!' The loss of his father had started a new perception of the world, one in which death might strike at any time. For some bereaved children the world is never completely secure again.

Linda was thoughtful when we looked back at the children's response to Ian's death and her own reactions. In retrospect, how did she see it? She told me:

'I think I've been too matter of fact. Thomas was hyperactive afterwards which wasn't helped by the fact that every time we seemed to go anywhere, it was full of people. Our house was always full of people. We had five holidays that year as well as weekends away. It was so busy that it might have been that which was the disruption for Thomas. Life was a whirl. I suppose it was to avoid thinking. I forced myself to go out every Saturday night.'

There was virtually no time to reflect and re-form the new family that Linda, Thomas and Helen had become.

Immediately after Ian's death Thomas used to tell people at school, 'My Dad's dead' in a kind of one-upmanship way, Linda thought. However both children wanted people to know. For example, a week after Ian's death a tiler came to the house to do some work, not a person they knew particularly well and Thomas said, in conversational tone, 'Do you know my Daddy is dead?' What might appear to be callously matter-of-fact was her son's way of coming to terms with his new status and informing the world at large.

In those ensuing months Thomas seemed obsessed by the idea that there were now three in the family and he was the only male. He would seek out friendships with other children where one parent was missing but, Linda remarked, he has recently stopped doing that, which she feels is a sign that he is coming to terms with his father's death.

Now, three years later, as the memory of their father fades, Thomas still refers to times 'when Daddy was alive' or sometimes when there is music playing on the radio, he will say 'Oh, is that another one that reminds you of Daddy?' 'Perhaps,' said Linda, 'I look wistful or sad, so he makes that connection.' He still asks about Ian's friends and colleagues, seeks details of his father's favourite cars and the mundane events that coloured his life. As new things happen to him Thomas asks if his father did them or asks Linda what she thinks Ian would have said about them. There is a need for him to check back. Helen, in contrast, asks few questions and seems to have no visual memory of her father.

Having worried endlessly about the effect of Ian's death on her children, Linda now feels that the worst is over. 'I think the children are well adjusted and are doing well at school and with friends. Thomas asked me recently why I don't have a boyfriend.' The reconciliation, the final acceptance, is tinged with sadness though, as it inevitably is and she knows the process of grieving and living with loss is a long term affair that has to be worked at each day at a time. She also realises that the process might have been easier for them all, if there had been the opportunity to talk to someone from outside the family. Someone who would listen, not judge, who would give time and not offer platitudes that 'everything was going to be all right' and who would let the children play out their worries instead of directing their activities at every opportunity. In efforts to help, friends and relatives, with the best will in the world, often block the expression of emotional distress and delay the grieving process. A professional counsellor working with Linda and her children would have provided this therapeutic support.

Despite her own great sorrow Linda encouraged her children to express their grief and to come through it. This is not always the case. How often do you hear people say 'Don't cry, everything will be all right' ? What they really mean is 'I can't cope with your tears, so stop and I won't feel so uncomfortable'. This response is unhelpful. It is crucial that children are encouraged to cry if they want to. Crying is a healthy, beneficial response to loss.

Anyone working with bereft children needs to develop the essential skill of active listening. We need to listen to what the child says, listen to their questions, listen to their needs. Only by actively listening can we really know what they want. This involves not only attention to their words but the tone of voice, the expression in their eyes, their actions, and their total body language. We must listen to 'the music behind the words'. Observe, be sensitive and responsive without being judgmental.

Children can face almost anything so long as they are told the truth and know that they can share their feelings with others who will comfort them. To express and share feelings is natural, yet often people unwittingly inhibit the child. If this happens the child becomes emotionally 'stuck'. By covering up their own emotions, parents or carers tell a child to hide their feelings, and give an unspoken message that this is the 'right' way to behave. Then, all too often when confronted with a child's reaction to grief, when they behave badly, have temper tantrums, are moody and seem not to care; those same adults become angry or distraught. Taken in by disturbing, superficial behaviour, they fail to see it as the child's way of expressing distress. They are not encouraged to talk about it so they find other outlets. Insensitive reactions create a further barrier which reduces effective communication.

What the child needs is time to grieve, as much as seven years some experts say, maybe a lifetime if not enough help is available in that formative learning time that is childhood. Any professionals involved in working in this area must help both the children themselves and their families to allow time and space for grief, acceptance and renewal.

Each child responds to loss from the basis of their own relationship with the person or thing that has been lost, depending on their own predispositions, personality, sensitivity and all the other factors that go to create each unique individual. In one sense, there are no hard and fast rules about how we help all children, but there are illuminating guidelines that highlight what helps and what hinders the process. Initially it is essential to accept that children mourn and that this can inflict a great strain on them. They need all our understanding and support to successfully weather the powerful waves of emotion that threaten to overwhelm them. Later, in Chapter 3, we will look at the process of grieving that children, like adults, experience, which culminates hopefully in a reconciliation and acceptance of the loss.

Throughout the book I consider what children themselves say about loss in their lives and take a lead from them rather than imposing received ideas. That has happened too often in the past and we still need to respect what our children tell us they feel, and to respond to what they tell us they need, if we are to successfully enable children to grow through loss. In the following chapters children speak directly of what loss means to them and let us know how we can empower them to face the suffering that is an integral part of life.

CHAPTER 2

Preparing for Loss

Children learn about loss very early. They see it on television, hear about it in stories and see that the natural world around them is full of birth and death. Every Christmas *The Snowman* is shown on British television. Raymond Briggs' (1978) enchanting story depicts the wonderful adventures of a little boy experiencing the magic world of the snowman who comes to life and transports him to the land where Father Christmas lives. Each year, we share the awful loss when the boy wakes to find the snowman gone. But why is this story so popular? One reason for its success is that it deals with the central human issues of wondrous life and sorrowful parting. and that rarely fails to move us. Children shed tears but know that the boy's life was richer for his wonderful experiences. They learn that the boy recovers from his sadness and returns to the love of his family. It is essentially a message of renewal and hope.

Much of children's literature is permeated with these themes of loss and survival and children love them precisely because they address their very deepest of feelings and most troubling fears. The most successful children's authors tell great stories and do not flinch in the face of pain, and it is useful for counsellors to make themselves aware of the wealth of material that is available. Judy Blume's writing tackles such diverse issues as divorce, abuse, step-parenting and children's anxieties about being different. In one notable story, *Blubber*, the heroine's anxieties revolve around being fat (Blume 1980). Anne Fine's brilliant book *Goggle Eyes* (Fine 1989), adapted for television, charts the child's view of her parents' separation, the introduction of her mother's new boyfriend and, after hellish episodes, the final acceptance of a new father figure. *I Am David* by Anne Holm, the powerfully compassionate story of a boy who escapes from a concentration camp and survives the terror, loneliness and fear that conflict imposes, delivers a final message of survival and hope (Holm 1979). Indeed, it is through the voices of these heroes that children can imagine surviving the utmost horror. Whilst some of these books are set in the past, as is *Goodnight Mister Tom* by Michelle Magorian, they speak of universal truths about love, hate, grief and joy and the unpredictability of human relationships (Magorian 1981).

Robert Swindells' *Stone Cold* (1993), winner of the Carnegie Award, directly confronts loss in the 1990s. Link, boy who is forced from home by a brutish stepfather, describes the world of the homeless and highlights fears that many young people have about their future. Perhaps the most significant characteristic about all of these books is that they point up fears and feelings that many adults would still prefer to deny. In becoming familiar with books that children read and with magazines that cater for specific age groups, you will learn more about what their preoccupations are and so prepare yourself for current concerns. Whatever the age of the child, there are books that enable them either to prepare for or cope with distressing personal life events.

Many public libraries have schemes that focus on 'difficult' issues. For instance Salford City Council (1997) have devised a delightfully illustrated pamphlet *Books For Special Situations*. These help parents or carers of younger children to explore such issues as adoption and fostering, death, feeling ill, starting school, staying away from home, disabilities and much more. Supportive initiatives such as this one, enable counsellors to access community facilities which can play a significant part in empowering parents and children. When you work with a family, if you can refer them to resources that are available in their local area, you help build links that may provide future support. Healthy learning about loss frequently starts with exposure to stories in books, in films and on television. If we can help children recognise and face such situations they will be better equipped to face personal loss encountered later.

Pets are an important part of this learning process since children are deeply attached to their animals, and the loss of a child's pet, or the class pet for that matter, can be extremely upsetting. By respecting the seriousness of this for the child, by understanding that it might be every bit as painful for them as losing a person, we introduce them to a healthy approach to handling grief.

Lorna's cat had been around for all of Lorna's twelve years. She loved her sixteen year old pet and was as sad when it died as she had been when her grandparents died:

At both these times, when my cat died and when my grandad and grandma died, I was deeply heartbroken and depressed and I will never forget them, ever! A girl at primary school said that I shouldn't get upset about my cat because, she said, 'It could be worse, your cat could have got run over.' That didn't help at all. I felt as if a bomb had gone off inside me.

Children do feel as though they are exploding with pain, that they might 'burst' as another child told me, because it feels so hard keeping all that hurt inside. By acknowledging the extent of their distress we allow children to grieve and set up healthy patterns of mourning which will stand them in good stead all of their life.

If a pet dies suddenly nothing can be done to soften the immediate impact of the blow, but where an animal is slowing down, its physical decline visible or where terminal illness is diagnosed, you can prepare children. We have a dog, Orly, who is now about 19, her birth date having got lost somewhere in my poor memory. She is slower than she used to be, gets up shakily on her frail legs and is very deaf. I am amazed that she still plods on, so I will not be shocked when she dies. Recognising these signs of infirmity about a year ago, it seemed right to talk to the children by way of preparation. At the time, Daniel who was then five, and Crystal, who was seven, bombarded me with questions: 'When will she die?, How will she die? Will we bury her in the garden, and if so where? And will the worms eat her?' Followed by, 'Can we put up a stone and write her name on it like we did with that dead red squirrel we found?' So it went on. After a while, questions answered as far as there were answers, self-interest came in: 'When Orly dies could we have a puppy? Could we have two, one for Daniel and one for me?'

I was not too surprised. Every child I have known has wanted a baby animal to take care of, usually a puppy or kitten. After all, my dog Orly has been part of the family longer than they have, and she does not do the silly antics they have seen pups perform. So now, a year later Orly is still here. I think she got a new lease of life when we got a puppy from the animal rescue league. In order to soften the blow of her death when it comes, we decided to get a younger dog now. That way there will not be an immediate yawning gap. It is, I admit, as much for my sake as theirs!

I realise not everyone has the space – or inclination – to include a younger dog by way of preparation, but preparing the child by talking and answering questions will help make the adjustment much easier when the time comes. Books can help too.

I'll Always Love You (1985) is the story of Elfie, 'the best dog in the world', and it tells how the family reacted to her death. All is spoken by the little boy who everyday told his dog 'I'll always love you Elfie' and was comforted when she died by the sure knowledge that his dog knew she was loved and would not be forgotten. This has implications for human relationships, as anyone working with children of dying parents or siblings knows that children may need help to express their love. Once love is given voice, the healing process for all involved is dramatically enhanced.

Parents sometimes believe that it is kinder to get an ailing pet put down while the child is out or sent away somewhere. Without any forewarning the child is met with a *fait accompli* when they come back to find the pet dead and buried so to speak, or in Andrew's case, given away. Andrew's dog did not die but the separation was just as hardfelt. Added to that pain was the serious blow to his trust struck by unthinking parents:

> I had a dog called Candy. It was a good dog but one night when I was going to bed a man knocked on the door. My Mum went to the door and let him in so I ran downstairs to see what was happening. There was a man talking about the dog and that was the last that I saw of my dog Candy.
>
> My Mum and Dad didn't tell me that the man was going to come and take my dog away and I wouldn't speak to them for a bit. It would have helped if my Mum and Dad had told me that the dog was going to someone else.

Andrew looked utterly miserable as he continued, 'If they had to give him away, why couldn't they have just told me? Instead I just had to watch.'

Significantly the loss of trust was the most damaging part of this experience. Andrew felt betrayed and his confidence in his parents was shattered. If they did it to him once they might do it again. They might lie or pretend about something else. And if that was the case, how could Andrew ever feel safe again? This is not to over-dramatise the situation as some people might think, it is to accept the reality of the boy's feelings and to acknowledge the depth of hurt.

Healing such wounds can only begin with the acceptance of the child's experiences. As a counsellor, the first point will be to provide a safe environment for the child to express such hurt, and to facilitate that dialogue between those involved if that is what the child wants. It is the counsellor's respectful, empathic acknowledgement of the child's pain that enables healing to begin. However, the child's trust may have been so badly dented that it may take a great deal of time before he can trust anyone else again. The breaking of trust causes a ripple that spreads far and wide, which is why it is so important to do everything in your power not to let children down. The 'kindness' of Andrew's parents, as we have seen, is not really so kind. Children need truthful explanations delivered sensitively.

Asking children about their experience of loss called forth many recollections about the deaths of animals, grandparents and other relatives. For some children, it was hard to admit that losing a pet was worse than the death of a relative. Some, like Simon, were defensive, fearing I might not appreciate just how sad it could be. Maybe like so many other children, he had experience of adults who trivialised his sorrow. He said: 'When I was about seven my Mum and Dad got rid of our dog who was called Max. I mean losing a dog might not sound much but he meant the world to me.'

Children feel keenly the manner of death of their pets. For Kathy, it was difficult to come to terms with her loss because she did not know what had finally happened to her hamster. It escaped from its cage when she was on holiday, whilst in the care of her big brother: 'After I had got over the shock, I was really angry. I could have killed my brother. He kept trying to cheer me up but I still felt angry. In the end it wore off, probably because he bought me another.' She added, 'I don't think I would have minded as much if it had died in its sleep, it was the way it died that really upset me.'

Where the circumstances of death are unusual or unknown reactions such as Kathy's are quite common. Where the body is not recovered, for example where life has been lost at sea or a body trapped in a mine shaft or an earthquake, bereavement is complicated by unanswered questions: 'What happened to him?', 'How did he die?', 'Was he disfigured?' or, the ultimate question, 'What if he didn't die? What if he's hurt somewhere with no one to look after him?' These questions reflect the thoughts that preoccupy the bereaved following 'abnormal' loss. Not knowing feels worse than the stark truth, however terrible that may be. For children this can apply as much to lost pets as it does to people.

It is therapeutic for children to say their own 'Goodbyes' to pets when they die. Some people feel it is wrong to let the dead body of a pet be seen, however if a child does want to see it, wherever possible, let them. Most children find it comforting to see and stroke their pet for one last time. Looking at the animal and touching it helps the child to learn the difference between the warm loving creature they have known and the lifeless corpse it has become. It shows them that it is not the breathing animal that is buried but the shell that has been left behind.

Holding a funeral service, saying a few words of celebration and farewell and putting up a marker, are important rituals for children as we saw in Thomas's experience in Chapter 1. All this is part of the healing process and helps the child accept that their pet has gone forever. Such early experiences, successfully managed, can provide a healthy armour against the shock of future loss. If such simple actions are allowed and encouraged a child is much more likely to handle other loss more successfully.

The run up to a stressful event is in itself stressful. If a child has been told that there is to be a separation, or that they are to go into hospital, or that someone close has a terminal illness, then the time may seem endless, especially to a very young child who has little concept of time. During such a waiting period, and later when the event actually takes place, a child will probably try to make sense of the situation by asking questions: 'Why is it going to happen?', 'What will happen next?', 'What will happen to me?'. The stress is eased if these are answered, not avoided. However many adults are worried that they cannot answer the questions adequately or without breaking down in some way.

If it is a question of factual information then books, as we noted earlier, can provide information, about what is entailed in facing cancer for instance. Hospitals have relevant material or videos that can be useful. However it is always important to make sure that the material is appropriate to the child's level of understanding and that the adult involved feels able to explore the issue. On the whole, it is better if the adult asked can answer the child's questions or seek the information they need though this is not always easy.

When counselling a family in this situation it is important to ask parents how they feel about sharing information with a child. In some instances, a distressed parent may prefer the counsellor to read such books or go through the material with the child. It can be very beneficial for the counsellor to do so with the parent(s) and child together; the presence of a third party to act as an anchor if anyone gets overwhelmed frequently reassures all concerned. Also parents may model their own future behaviour on the counsellor's approach, so expanding their own skills of listening and empathy for instance. What is important is that the child's questions are accepted and answered even when there is no definite, unequivocal answer.

Time can seem endless when the child is waiting for someone they love to return. When Jeff's wife left him with one daughter aged ten months and Katherine, who was two-and-a-half he found it almost impossible to explain her absence. He told me, 'Katherine was asking where her Mummy was all the time, and when she would be coming back. I hinted it would be a long time and she associated the summer with a long time. I told her one morning a few months later that her Mummy would not be coming back. She ran away. She was only three years old and she tried to run away down the street.'

Well-intentioned inaccurate information created false hope for Katherine. Though Jeff's position was extremely difficult, if you are working with someone in a similar situation, every effort should be made to tell the child the true facts. Misinformation causes delayed, additional distress.

Breaking bad news is never easy though Mark's mother and father tried to prepare him. Aged twelve he recalled the events:

When I was nine my Mum and Dad got a divorce. They told me weeks before my Mum left my Dad. I was hoping to wake up and find that it was all a bad dream but I didn't. My Mum was understanding but I was still upset. I saw my Dad every week and we enjoyed ourselves, but part of our relationship was gone.

We will examine ways in which children react to loss later in the book, but at this point it is important to acknowledge that children like Mark need a lot of time to come to terms with endings they experience. It is what the endings give rise to that further distresses many children. Twelve-year-old Aron was very distraught during the break up of his parents' marriage because, as he said 'I thought I'd have to take most of the pain because they'd ask me who I wanted to live with and I'd have to decide.' He was confused and scared that he would not know what was the 'right' decision. Yet, how could there be a 'right' decision for Aron when he loved both his parents and did not want to choose between them?

Counsellors in mediation services can offer enormous help to families like Aron's. They provide an opportunity for separating parents to make decisions about difficult areas such as contact arrangements and financial details. With knowledge of the law as well as using specialist arbitration skills, the counsellor facilitates communication between all parties involved so that negotiations do not become too acrimonious. The best interests of the child(ren) are at the heart of such mediation processes and though marriages may not be saved, the mediation can limit the damage. Whilst the children may not be involved in all sessions, for instance when the parents want to decide who should file for a divorce and when, children should be invited to contribute wherever possible.

As a counsellor you should be prepared to see children separately from their parents, either with siblings or alone if they are happy to do so. This gives them an opportunity to express their own views, to identify areas of concern and a chance to ask questions they may not be able to put at home. It is crucial that children are involved in the decision-making process about their future without being overburdened by responsibility. Ultimately the child will not take the decision, but his views must be heard and when the adults do decide what is in the best interests of the child, they need to be able to explain the reasons for their decisions.

A mediation counsellor needs to be available for some time after the final settlement so that children can be supported as they come to terms with new arrangements and adjustments. Thirteen-year-old Fiona told me that she and her brother found such continued support really helpful, especially since her grandparents were upset themselves and there was no else to talk to. She explained that her younger brother, who had been the class 'toughie' until their parents separation, burst out crying in the playground one day. He was not only grieving for his absent father, but crying because he knew he had lost his place with the other children in his primary school. His image would never be the same again. Fiona said that all the other children laughed at him, calling him a 'cry baby' and seemed to revel in his distress. At the conciliation offices Fiona and her brother could talk freely about such incidents and their conflicting feelings, knowing they would be listened to and taken seriously.

Mediation encourages parents to thoroughly consider the outcome of their decisions so that they can separate in a responsible way. Users to whom I spoke at the Newcastle Upon Tyne office were unanimously praiseworthy. No one denied the difficulties, the painful moments, the times they felt like never coming back, but they did go back and all agreed it helped them make better adjustments for life after divorce. They felt more prepared having taken time to talk through their options and feelings in a way that valued each member involved in the process.

Separation does not stop feelings of hurt, so it is ludicrous to expect children to bounce back to 'normal' once a divorce or separation has taken place. Children may continue to feel as though they are walking a tightrope. Battles over who should live where and with whom and de-stabilising shifts of allegiance within the family as blame is apportioned, disturb the child's balance. Life goes out of kilter. And because of this some children sacrifice their own relationships with one parent in order to stop the agony, either their own or that of the parent who is obviously not coping with whatever arrangements have been made, about access for instance. Children like these, who are caught in the middle between two parents they love, often experience overwhelming stress, which is why mediation is so important for children.

Counsellors involved in the mediation process encourage parents to avoid using children in their own matrimonial conflict. As the only joint asset that cannot be split, the child all too often becomes the focal point of the struggle for power and retribution between the partners. Confusion may arise in the child who is forced to reject one parent in favour of the other, or to protect one from the other. Whilst all these aspects have to be worked through, it is also important to recognise the amount of self-blame and guilt that children take on when parents split up. It is an issue we will return in some depth in Chapter 4.

There are other experiences of loss that almost all children face. However the fact of their universality does not lessen the impact on the child. Transition from primary school to secondary school is something almost every child experiences but for the sensitive, more anxious child, this can be a time of great challenge. The secure intimacy of a small school often gives way to a large impersonal building which seems to be a maze of corridors and staircases. The child feels unsure of the routine, the expectations, his new teachers and fellow pupils. In addition he may have heard rumours prior to the changeover. Acute anxiety about changing schools may force children to truant, run away, or ultimately to become school-phobic, so it is important to ease early anxieties wherever possible.

Any transition can be especially difficult for the child who, perhaps because of illness, misses the first few days or weeks of the new school year, or who transfers mid-term. By the time he arrives, friendship groups are established and he feels the outsider, the marginal one. This causes real distress and makes it more difficult for him to establish himself. Schools need to be aware of this and organise a class welcome group to ease in the latecomer.

Preparing children for expected stress is important but often when a child is distressed the signals go unrecognised, or we misread the signs and communication breaks down. It is to this area of communication that we now turn in Chapter 3.

CHAPTER 3

'Then Everything Changed'

I saw my brother on a life support machine. He looked just like a battered doll. He was knocked down on his way to school. He was three years older than me, I was eleven… I just fought back the anger and pain. I just helped my Mum and Dad through it. They didn't seem to notice how I was feeling, but five years have gone by now and I am still angry, confused and sad. I can't talk about this to anyone because if I say anything to Mum I'll upset her, and the same with Dad.

Rosemary, now sixteen years old

Children have the right to be taken seriously, respected and understood. Yet again and again children like Rosemary have told me that their feelings were not noticed let alone respected. An isolating veil of silence shields sorrows and forms a yawning gap between the child's feelings and the response of the rest of their community.

A child experiences a profound sense of loss, grief and anxiety when someone they love dies or leaves, particularly a parent, since young children invest almost all their emotional energy in their parents. Feelings of emptiness, tearfulness, and aching fatigue take over. Where there has been divorce or a natural disaster, although no one has died the intact family or the world the child knew has 'died'. For the child the world they knew has perished and will never be the same again. And whilst children may not have 'adult' language to express their emotions it does not mean that they do not feel: limited vocabulary does not mean limited feelings. In the next three chapters we will see how children reveal their stress, and then we will discover strategies that facilitate growth and renewal.

The first task in dealing with loss is finding the words to say it. What language do you use to tell a child someone they love is dead or is leaving? Anxious to break the news of a death as gently as possible, we may in fact set up further anxieties for children by using familiar words in unfamiliar contexts.

Using euphemisms instead of plain words that state the truth causes confusion, as John's experience testifies.

When her father died Mary told her son John that his grandfather had 'gone to sleep'. This euphemism was taken literally by the five year old. He did not ask 'When will he wake up?' as other children might; had he done so the ensuing misunderstanding could have been avoided. What did happen was that John became afraid to sleep in case the same thing happened to him. Bedtimes became a struggle and John would often be wide awake when his mother and father were going to bed. Eventually, eyes dark ringed, John told his mother why he was afraid to sleep, and she clarified her words and reassured her son that when he went to sleep he would not die.

This attempt to soften the blow of death is often inscribed on gravestones: 'Asleep in the arms of Jesus', 'Gently Sleeping in Heaven' and so on. Children who have visited cemeteries read the words and may subsequently harbour erroneous ideas about the nature of death and dying. I often think that the reason people fear being buried alive stems from this early mis-information. Imagine being told that your favourite Grandma has fallen asleep and is going to be buried. I would be frightened and puzzled and terrified that these grown-ups might bury me too if I fall asleep. I would worry about how Grandma would breathe in that dark hole, and wonder why they were doing it to her. Certainly, fear of sleeping is not uncommon for a child following the death of someone close.

Particularly where intense emotions are involved it is vital that the information is clearly communicated. The language used is of critical importance. It should be plain, simple and jargon free. The caring tone of voice, reassuring body language and willingness to answer questions, will give the child more reassurance than trying to fudge the unpalatable truth. When children do not understand what has happened or are confused by the information, they are more likely to be apprehensive and fretful. Typically they may cling more to the adults left behind, especially where a parent has died. Seek to clarify understanding by sensitive questioning and gentle restatement of the truth. The child will accept what they are capable of taking in at the time, and if trust has been established, will be willing to ask questions in future when they need more information.

Catherine, now forty years old, was given the news of her mother's death with brutal abruptness, and I have included her words to emphasise how *not* to break such news to a child, and how *not* to manage the situation subsequently. Catherine still finds handling any kind of loss too much to cope with and, not surprisingly given this experience, she withdraws behind a wall of silence:

I was seven years old when my mother died. I went to school that morning as usual. She had been ill for some time, in and out of hospital but never in bed for any length of time. All I knew was that she had a 'poorly arm' and had it in a sling. (Later I found out she suffered from breast cancer.)

Mid-morning the head teacher came and took me outside the classroom and told me I was to go to a neighbour's house for lunch. When I got there this neighbour I had always called 'Aunty' told me my mother had died and I was to go back to school in the afternoon. When I arrived home later that afternoon, all the curtains were closed and my Gran met me in the hall telling me that I should not go into the parlour. I wasn't told why but they said I would be a naughty girl if I did. I only learned later in life that she had been laid out in there. Her death was never spoken of to me. I felt I couldn't ask. I don't remember much about her and wasn't encouraged to ask.

A few weeks after her death my Gran, who we lived with, also died of cancer but I cannot remember much about this except that my father and I went to live with his sister as the house had to be sold.

Catherine remembers no comforting consolation, no explanations and no chance to openly grieve. How closely is her present depression linked to that time? How might her pain have been recognised?

Reactions to death are very similar to those at other times of loss, and whilst they may be more intense what is critical is the importance of that loss to the individual child. There are three main stages of mourning:

Phase 1 – Early Grief: the Protest phase

Phase 2 – Acute Grief: the Disorganisation phase

Phase 3 – Subsiding Grief: the Re-organisation phase.

These stages are not rigid – each person grieves in their own unique way – but they act as a guide to reactions you might encounter. However, a child may seem to be at one stage one day yet revert to another the next, so do not expect an easily recognisable progression. Grieving is a process not a linear pathway and there is no set pattern. Children range through the same emotions of grieving as do adults even though they may express them in different ways. The age of the child makes a difference too.

Very young children have a limited comprehension of the permanence of death, but recognise it as separation and may react with profound sadness. Five to eight year olds are in the stage of 'magical thinking', believing that wishing can make something happen. They may for instance be horror-stricken by their apparent power to make an event take place if they earlier wished it to happen. For example, if a child wished that a sibling would hurt themself, and the child is then injured, the child holds a belief that they have caused the event to happen. The continued belief in this magical power is apparent in children's behaviour. Sometimes they become especially good and conscientious, hoping they might bring about a recovery, or where there has been a death, hoping for a resurrection.

Children between the ages of eight and ten are often intrigued by death. Death is sometimes seen as a person who comes to get them, for example a ghost or death is a consequence, for example a punishment for thinking or doing something wrong. One ten-year-old girl, blaming herself, said, 'If I had stayed off school and looked after Mum, she wouldn't have died.' From about the age of nine, children begin to grasp the permanency of death and express grief as adults do.

Phase 1 – The Protest Phase

Feeling of *shock, alarm, numbness* and *denial* are common at first. The initial shock of separation and loss shows itself physically as well as emotionally. Physical changes include increased heart rate, muscular tension, sweating, dryness of the mouth, bowel and bladder relaxation and breathing changes, for example shortness of breath or continual deep sighing.

Such reactions may come in waves of a few moments or can last for hours, and the grieving child feels weakened and exhausted to such an extent that everything is too much of an effort and they feel unable to carry on. At this stage the child should be given opportunities to rest. It helps to explain that coming to terms with sadness and loss uses up a lot of energy, and that their tiredness is not a threat but a natural response to what has happened. Grieving is hard work.

In some instances the child appears to have no reaction to the traumatic news of loss. As Rosemary said when her father told her of her brother's sudden death, 'I didn't cry because I didn't believe him'. The child may continue to talk about the dead person in the present tense and ask when he will be back. On immediately receiving the news a child may, like Rosemary, react casually, seemingly unmoved by the event. The extreme shock causes numbness. Anyone working with families at this time can assist by explaining that children need time for the full implications of loss to sink in.

First superficial impressions of a child's reaction to loss can be very deceptive. The calm exterior often belies a frightened, shocked child stunned into numbness. They sense a major alteration taking place which will change their life for ever. In part this alarm is raised by changes in the behaviour of the adults closest to them, be they parents, neighbours or friends of the family. Subtle changes, alterations in the way parents talk to each other – or don't – or differences such as tone of voice, body language and moods, all tell the child that something is amiss. They take in all the information and are afraid of what may happen. The as-yet-unknown feels ominous.

When we are faced with trauma, emotional or physical, an in-built protective mechanism comes into play. It screens out devastating material so that we do not get overloaded, and instead deals with what we are capable of coping with at that time. Thus, a child's first reaction to a parent's death or sudden admission to hospital may be 'Who will take me to school tomorrow?' Concentration on practicalities gives a focus and shifts feelings from the pain and shock to commonplace 'doing'. (You can compare this to adults, like Linda whose husband Ian died, who seem to manage very well immediately after a death when they are fully taken up with arranging practical things such as getting the death certificate or arranging the funeral. However, as soon as all that activity is over they have to deal with their feelings of loss.)

Later the child may go through the daily motions of living in a robot-like fashion. They may be lacking in energy, smile mechanically without showing true feeling or seem out of tune with what is going on around them. Such emotionally flat behaviour is often interspersed with sudden outbursts of anger or tears. Seeing a child so withdrawn can be very distressing for those around, but it is often symptomatic of this early stage of grieving, and may last for hours or weeks. However upsetting for the onlookers, it is important to understand that for the bereaved child it is a form of protection.

Feelings of numbness often alternate with anger or distress as the loss begins to register, physical symptoms such as nervous excema and enuresis may appear or become aggravated. In terms of behaviour, boys are generally more likely to become hyperactive and aggressive whilst girls tend to be more clinging and withdrawn. There may be intense pining, heightened irritability and crying aloud for the lost person. In many cultures this crying aloud, or 'keening', is actively encouraged. It is a very therapeutic way to give vent to the powerful emotions churning inside.

Children depend on adults to look after them, to feed and clothe them and to keep them safe. The loss of a family member threatens this protective security and causes the child to feel vulnerable. Fergal, who was very close to his Grandmother and sought her home as an escape from his own when she was alive, greeted the news of her death with, 'What am I going to do now Nana's dead. I've nowhere to go.' He was bereft not of place – though that was the easiest to pinpoint – but of her care, unconditional acceptance and total loyalty. No one else in his world gave him that. Emotionally as well as physically this teenage boy had 'nowhere to go'. 'Who is going to look after me?' was the unconscious cry of alarm.

This unconscious alarm that children feel calls for adult action. Children will need to be reassured that just because one death has happened it does not mean that more are on the way. One five-year-old whose sister had died asked his Mum, 'Is it my turn to die next?' Intense fears of death peak at around five or six years of age – but remember that all children are different and these ages are merely guidelines. If bereavement occurs at this time look out for this kind of 'multiplication' idea. Signs that they may be present can be seen in increased clingy behaviour, fear of going out of sight of the adults they care about, disinclination to go to nursery or school and wanting to sleep in parents' or siblings' beds. This severe *separation anxiety* can lead to depression and physical ill health, but usually the early panic subsides after reassurance and time. Comforting physical closeness and safety, in familiar places with familiar people, will help enormously.

Another sign of the alarm response is insomnia. One explanation is that our body is still in a state of heightened alertness, prepared to guard against further danger. Loss is a major threat. It endangers our known world and can be a threat to our own survival. 'How can I bear it?' we ask ourselves, 'How can I carry on?'. When trust in your world is shaken it can be difficult to let down your guard enough to sleep. Also, disturbing dreams may cause some children further anxiety (more of dreams in Chapter 5).

In an atmosphere of tension, be it because of illness, family strife or anxiety, children may be afraid to ask what is going on in case it leads to a telling off. Somehow, by not asking direct questions, children feel they can avoid the ultimate terrible truth, whatever they imagine it to be. Twelve-year-old Christine was confused by events surrounding her parents divorce, as she graphically describes:

When I was five and my brother was three our parents split up. It was a very upsetting time for me because we weren't allowed to see our Mum. My brother didn't really know what was going on but I knew. But the bit I didn't understand was why we couldn't see our Mum and why my Mum and Dad had to keep going to court.

After about two years we were allowed to see our Mum every weekend but we had to stay with our Dad during the week. Then my Dad met a girl called Jean. One night my brother and me were upstairs getting ready for bed when my Mum walked in to see us. She was coming upstairs when my Dad heard her and he came out. He wouldn't let my Mum up the stairs to see us so my Mum got hold of my Dad's hair and started pulling it. He got hold of my Mum and threw her down the stairs. By this time I was crying my eyes out and screaming for my Mum. I wouldn't let my Dad touch me, or anyone else for that matter.

When I had settled down a bit, Jean comforted me and I was all right. My Dad told me we had to live with him and we could see our Mum once a fortnight. We still live like that now, eight years later, but because I am older I miss my Mum more. Sometimes I feel like running away and going to live with her, but my dad needs me more than my Mum does.

Christine's mother had come round that night because she had just found out that her ex-husband was trying to reduce the amount of contact time she had with her children. The result was a scene Christine has never forgotten. And now, eight years later, she continues to live with the conflict of wanting to live with both her parents. What she has opted for is the sacrificing of her own desire to live with her mother, in order to stay with the adult who 'needs' her most. This reversal of caring roles, where the child takes care of the perceived emotional needs of the parent, has significant implications for later relationships. Inability to legitimately state what they want forces many children to subsume their needs in future adult relationships, which in turn may lead to depression, chronic poor health and abusive relationships.

Phase 2 – The Disorganisation Phase

Anger usually surfaces in this acute stage of mourning as the reality of the loss sinks in. Children may seek to blame someone – the doctor, their parent, even the deceased. Such strong feelings can be very hard to bear especially if the child uses the immediate family members as the butt of their intense anger. 'I hate you! I wish you had died instead of Daddy' may be thrown out in a furious, violent reaction to loss. However, for that child it is part of the process they have to go through in order to come through the harrowing trauma. If you explain this to the remaining family members with whom you are working, it will help them not to take such remarks personally and will enable them to accept them without feeling guilty, especially since they too may believe that the 'wrong' person died.

Anger is a completely natural response to loss of any kind – a constructive and active reaction to feelings of powerlessness. It is at the very least a sign of strong energy, of life force which if harnessed can be a drive to ensure survival. What is more natural than to feel angry that we cannot control what has happened to us? How understandable it is that we turn anger on ourselves for failing to prevent the death of someone we love. The acceptance of a child's anger at this time is particularly important since it acts as a catharsis (Kubler-Ross 1980).

Aggression signals that the child is undergoing strain. After a divorce, it is likely to be aimed at the parent with whom the child spends most time.

Unprovoked temper tantrums interspersed with crying bouts and rebelliousness – above the norm of course – can be hellish. For professionals who do not live within the family for twenty-four hours a day it is important to empathise with the difficulties. A child who refuses to go to bed at their usual time, swears and throws things around, refuses to do homework or usual family chores, creates tension for all who share their space, and it is difficult for them to bear in mind that the provocative behaviour may well be a stress reaction.

The child's family may find it particularly difficult when the anger felt about the event is disguised, or displaced onto siblings so that constant fights become the order of the day. Anger is a form of defensive behaviour. By becoming angry and difficult with those around them children outwardly display their inner turmoil. The outer chaos they create mirrors their inner storm. Sensitivity to the child's vulnerability and increased needs should be emphasised, the anger the child feels is not easy for him or her either.

Two-year-old Henry stopped talking when his father left to work abroad. At first his mother Jan thought it was his way of dealing with the shock of not having his father at home, but did not really believe that her son was bothered about the change. However, a few days later when Henry began banging his head against the bars of his cot, badly bruising his head, she had to think again. Jan mistakenly thought that small children are unaffected by loss really. Her son's pain and rage were quite apparent in his behaviour although he could not talk about those feelings.

Many children express distress not in words but in behaviour. Out of the blue the child may become an unpredictable, infuriating little tyrant, seemingly closed to all reasoning. The distressed and distressing child frequently has mood swings which follow no discernible pattern. When faced with a child who puzzles and frustrates, we must first ask if it is typical behaviour for a child of that age. For example, when five-year-old Paula's parents divorced she seemed to take it quite well. Her behaviour was just as before except for one thing – she kept asking about her father, showing great interest in his welfare. She would say things like 'I hope Daddy doesn't get too tired and crash his car' or 'Do you think Daddy will have finished his work now?' On and on she would prattle.

Paula's mother was very irritated, seeing these questions as a deliberate attempt to annoy her, and in turn was furious with Paula. What she did not know was that her daughter was taking a new developmental step. Asking these kinds of questions are part of the normal development of a child of that age who is beginning to be more aware of the outside world and more concerned about other people. Whilst Paula was behaving perfectly normally for a child her age, taking the change of circumstance in her stride, other children are not so tolerant. As we will see later, others find development delayed because of a particularly stressful life event.

Guilt is often a co-traveller with anger in the grieving process. The child may believe that something they did or did not do contributed towards the death. This was brought home to me recently when a man told me that for years he thought that he had caused his father's death because he had left his toys on the floor. His father died suddenly of a heart attack and his body lay across the strewn toys in the kitchen. As a five-year-old Peter was terrified that it was his fault and was far too scared to tell his mother lest something dreadful happen to him too. Like Peter, other children feel they cannot reveal their sense of guilt in case it causes further problems, so they carry the burden alone. When Fran's dog was accidently run over it left her with a dilemma: 'I let it off the lead and the next thing I knew it was lying dead in the road. I was trapped because I did not want to go home and tell my parents because it was my fault.' Feelings of guilt may lead to brooding withdrawal.

Another manifestation of anger may be seen in *rejection*. The child may disown the absent parent because they feel rejected, particularly where suicide was the cause of death. The child defends themself against the loss by denying they ever cared: 'I don't care whether he's here or not, I never liked him anyway.' These mixtures of anger and denial are more pieces in the jigsaw puzzle that make up the mourning picture.

Denial and disbelief

As we have seen, some children do not accept that loss has happened or they sometimes 'forget'. In daydreams and night dreams the child senses the presence of the dead person so convincingly that they cannot believe that they are not there anymore. This denial, 'No, it's not true. He can't be dead.' is our earliest defence when death strikes. At its simplest level infants use it when they cover their eyes and look away, children do it at bedtime when they see the clock and say 'Oh no, the clock is wrong. It can't be that time'. Some denial is conscious but a great deal is not.

For many children denial and escape into fantasy is the only way to ease their pain. There is an Arab proverb, 'We cannot look at the sun all the time. We cannot face death all the time.' Children need space to look away from the trauma otherwise their very survival seems under threat.

Denial can problematic for the others involved but it shows that the child is capable of building strong emotional bonds and has accepted love. In the midst of all the anguish of loss it gives good hope for the future, and augers well for the possibility of new bonds and new love. Additionally fantasies may be part of the child's coping strategy. For example, fantasies of children whose parents have divorced frequently revolve around the whole family getting back together again. Continued longing for a reconciliation of the family is common, even years later when their parents have married new partners. Ten year old Stephanie's recurring dream reflects this, 'Somehow, Mum and Dad forgot the past and just rewound back to where all the happy times were.'

Another common fantasy concerns the parent who has left following separation. In it the father – it is still usually the case that the child stays with the mother – sadly sits alone in an empty room needing the solace that only his child can bring. This imagined scenario makes the child feel wanted and less rejected, but also brings attendant feelings of guilt and sorrow. This self-punishment is founded on the child's belief that they could have prevented the separation. This is not helped of course if the absent parent plays up the 'poor me' role at the child's expense.

Other children fantasise the opposite, that the absent parent is having a wonderful time and giving their love to other people, particularly other children. Eleven-year-old Prudence feels left out by her father, and jealous too: 'My sisters and me just wish he would find some way of showing he cares for us. Now he has met another woman who has a son and daughter. I don't like that at all because they make sure my Dad loves and takes more care of them.' She longs for the day he will return but notice how she does not blame her father for his lack of interest but his new partner and her children. It is too painful to admit that your parent does not come up to your expectations, much easier and safer to blame the stranger. Unfortunately, the barriers raised against her fathers' new partner will probably make it difficult for Prudence to build any relationship with this new family in future, and will probably decrease contact even further – the cycle of alienation is under way.

Hyperactivity can be a way of denying loss. Non-stop chattering, endless fidgeting, constantly on the go and never seeming to relax, are signs of hyperactive behaviour. Not to be confused with an ordinary lively child, such children are generally exhausting to be with and seem unable to stop their endless frenetic activity. Following a bereavement, such hyperactivity ensures that the child does not have time to think about their loss. It is a physical acting out of their mental avoidance. Just as a workaholic stops themself thinking about their difficult marriage, a play-aholic child keeps their fear and pain at bay by unceasing activity and noise. These children may have difficulties being alone. They want constant playmates, the television on or a story tape, any activity to keep their mind off what has happened. The continued presence of a caring adult who will find time to listen and play can be of enormous benefit to such a child.

Occasionally a child's development seems to have stopped altogether or regressed to an earlier developmental stage. A child may become emotionally 'frozen', unable or unwilling to use emotional energy to move from their 'stuck' position. The child may fail to thrive, fail to gain the appropriate height and weight for their age, so that physical growth appears to have stopped altogether; long term this could lead to psycho-social-dwarfism. Another child may regress to an earlier form of behaviour, play or language, adopting a squeaky voice or baby talk, harking back to a former stress-free time.

Play with other children may change. They may be unable to play successfully with others and prefer solitary activities. Of course, this may be a temporary reaction to the strain, but here we are talking about sustained periods of time, as it was for three-year-old Seth. When his brother had to go into hospital, Seth's anxiety was clear. He developed a skin rash, lost interest in his food, and his usual toys held no pleasure for him. In his listlessness all he wanted was to sit on his mother's knee being held closely and quietly as he had when he was a baby.

Regression caused by excessive anxiety is fairly easy to spot. Bedwetting is a common sign and if a child has been dry at night in the past but regresses in this way, explain that this does happen when people are going through a hard time, and that sometimes even adults do it. Offer reassurance that it will stop as life settles down again. In the case of toddlers who have not yet established dry nights, warn the parents to be prepared for it to take longer, such delays are not uncommon.

Chronic bedwetting causes great distress. Twelve-year-old David said, 'I try to keep it a secret. I don't go to stay with friends and I can't go to camp in case anyone finds out. When I was seven someone at school found out and they called me "smelly" and "wee-face."' Parents sick of changing beds every morning understandably lose patience and tell the child to stop it. The child, who cannot control the enuresis, then feels guilty because they think they should be able to, and feel a failure since no-one else talks about having that difficulty.

Research has shown that next to crying wetting is the most commonly stated reason for non-accidental injury to children (Kemp 1972). The national organisation ERIC (Eneuresis Resource and Information Centre) offers an information service, ideas, counselling and alarm pads, as well as a booklet for children to let them know that they are not alone and that they can learn bladder control.

Feeding problems, nail biting, sleep disturbance and bad dreams, as well as increased allergic responses such as excema or asthma, are all stress signs to look out for. Particularly with younger children you can see thumb-sucking, rocking to and fro, wanting to be fed soft foods and needing to be held close much of the time, like Seth, are subconscious reminders of less traumatic times. It is a child's way of comforting themselves, of having some control in a world which feels out of control.

Part of the grieving process involves longing for the past, yearning and pining for what might have been if only this terrible blow had not struck. Many children's books and films deal with this theme of loss and restitution: *Star Wars*, *The Wizard of Oz*, *ET*, *Oliver* and *Beauty And The Beast* are just a few. Not all the stories have a happy ending – Darth Vader does not renounce the evil empire until faced with death so our hero Luke Skywalker has to live all his life without his natural father. However, in the best of these myths and stories there is some kind of resolution and growth towards maturity, and an acceptance that life's lessons are not always easy to learn.

This outgrowth from yearning requires the child to seek the loved one who is gone. With a very young child whose father has died say, this is revealed by the child looking in places their father used to frequent. They scan the horizon, react to the noise of a car pulling up, as if expecting their father to arrive, but the lonely vigil does not bring the loved one back. As death is a totally alien concept for the very young child it is hard for them to grasp that the dead person will not return. In older children, there is the hope against hope that there has been a mistake and that they will wake up from a bad dream and find everything back to normal. It takes time for the loss to be accepted. Impatience with a child who is preoccupied with searching can delay rather than facilitate grieving. The child is compelled to go through their own process of hoping and searching.

Finally, through repeated unsuccessful searching, the child will give up the quest. The acceptance of the finality of their loss and 'letting go' is usually very sad but indicates progression towards the last phrase of mourning which we will look at in the next chapter.

CHAPTER 4

Coming to Terms

Phase 3 – The Re-Organisation Phase

In this final phase of grieving there is a conflict between the need to 'let go' in an emotional sense and the wish to hold on. This pull between the known past and the unknown future is the keynote to resolution of grief.

Acceptance is the culmination of the taxing process in which the child comes to accept the reality of the loss and their feelings about what has happened. They begin to adjust successfully. They can look forward to events in the future and recognise that whilst their time with the dead person has ended, memories live on. The bereaved person is unlikely to forget the anguish but it will become a sad memory rather than a constantly painful wound. After winter comes spring. Recovery from grief is natural and by helping children to understand that accepting the loss is *not* a betrayal of the deceased person, they are much more likely to move on to this final stage.

Signs of stress may be more overt at this point. Physically the child's health may suffer with increased susceptibility to minor ailments – colds, sore throats, stomach upsets and fatigue. We know from recent developments in psychoneuroimmunology that stress reduces the effectiveness of the immune system making the body less resistant to illness (Martin 1997). Depression and/or strong feelings of helplessness lower our body's resistance to infection and depletes our immune defence system. After a major loss increased sickness, be it organic or psychosomatic in nature, must be handled with care. When children get the attention they need they will become stronger on all fronts and return to good health once more.

The early resolution of grief enables children to avoid long-term psychological ill-health. Many men and women I have worked with in counselling have come to understand that their adult tears were really in response to events in the past that they had been told to dismiss or deny. Children's tears will help to cleanse the pain and heal the hurt, and all who work with children have a responsibility to facilitate that expression. Crying releases tension and helps safeguard the child against lasting trauma: tears are cathartic. However, we also need to be aware of our own attitudes to grief and tears and aware of the impact our body language makes, even a slight move away from a child in crisis will be interpreted as a signal that their emotions are unacceptable.

It is helpful to listen to what children say about their experience of this process. Twelve-year-old Lucy is mad about horses. She helps muck out at a nearby stable and goes riding there too. When she started riding three years ago, she encountered Min:

> I began to ride this beautiful grey, Welsh mountain pony. She was very pretty and taught me exactly the perfect friendship of a girl and a horse...much later, Min caught a cold. It may not sound serious but Min was an old pony. I was assured that she would be fine. She wasn't and she died. Naturally I was deeply upset but it helped to look at pictures. Memories of her and even looking at logs I used to jump over with her made me feel better; also I took some of her grey hair out of her old Dandy brush. It didn't help when I got sympathy from the other girls at the stables because I would burst into tears again. All I wanted was to be left on my own so I could have a good cry all to myself. To do this I would – and I still do – take a wheelbarrow full of muck, go to the muck heap and cry by myself.

In her special place Lucy has the space to grieve in peace and quiet, a point that is useful to bear in mind when working with children. Help the child to identify a safe, discreet place where their privacy will be respected.

There are many other reactions to loss that a child may have which become apparent at this stage, for instance increased fears about death. Many children go through a phase in which they worry that a member of their family is going to die or that they themselves are about to die. Intimations of mortality are hard to come to terms with at any age, but when a child realises that death is something that could happen to them, it is frightening. Clearly if a child has a serious, life threatening illness, the anxiety is firmly based in reality, but where there is no linked cause it is useful to help the child to discover the roots of their anxieties. They may have heard rumours or tall tales at school and be labouring under ill-informed delusions. Honest answers to questions, and sensitive discussions will do a great deal to dispel irrational fears.

Children who have been inadequately prepared for loss or misled about it may develop severe anxiety about death. Anita, aged thirteen, had not been told of her mother's impending death. No-one had spoken of the probable affects of her mother's cancer. When her mother died, Anita was shocked rigid. She developed a terror of unexpected death, was afraid to go to sleep, afraid of taking part in sport lest she be injured and die. She regularly examined her body for any signs of illness that could be likened to her mother's and was less and less able to function normally. A school counsellor recognised that Anita was in need of help, and counselling helped her to eventually resolve her shock and grief. It freed her to live without the fear of death overshadowing her every moment (Tatelbaum 1981).

As we have seen earlier fears for health may preoccupy a child following a loss. Some children begin to suffer from hypochondria, indeed they may show physical symptoms similar to those the parent had before death. Or the child may have other, more generalised ailments: unconsciously the child may find asking for help for physical ailments easier than asking for help to ease emotional pain. For the remaining parent also it can often be easier to respond practically to illness than to manage raw, emotional hurt.

The mourning that follows bereavement, in whatever form, is not an illness but a process that has to run its course. Throughout that process the child needs to know that they are not alone, so a close, caring adult should be identified as an anchor, be this a family member, friend, teacher, social worker – whoever seems most appropriate given the individual circumstances of the child. There is no short-cut to easing the pain of loss, and the child needs to know their feelings are normal and part of living.

Making sense of loss is the task children must face at whatever age they experience it, and it is particularly daunting when a child's sibling dies. The impact of a child's death is enormous. Jewett reports that in about half the families in which a child dies, one or more siblings will develop symptoms such as depression, severe separation anxiety or school problems (Jewett 1984). However, this seems linked to changes in the parents' behaviour rather than the death itself. These changes may lead to marital breakdown. The imposed strain is too hard for some parents to bear, though in other cases it knits the couple more closely together. Parents and their remaining children may be devastated by the death of a child in the family and all need sensitive care and support to overcome such a catastrophic experience.

The love/hate relationships and sibling rivalry that many brothers and sisters have complicates their reactions. Feelings of guilt are almost inevitable when a sibling dies. As we saw earlier, until around the age of eight children often blame themselves, because in play or in their imagination they have wished their sibling dead. They might have shouted in anger, 'I wish you were dead' or 'Drop dead'. If death actually occurs they then feel in some way responsible and therefore guilty. Such feelings are intensified if they feel left out by parents who cannot do much more than cope with their own grief. We can help by acknowledging the feelings and explaining that those thoughts and angry words played no part in the death. Asking the child to give examples of wishes that have not come true may go some way to dispelling this belief in their own 'magical power'.

SIBS is a group for bereaved teenagers who meet once a month at the Alder Centre at the Alder Hospital, Liverpool. The centre was set up to help anyone affected by the death of a child, and as well as offering a place to talk it provides counselling and support groups. Thirteen-year-old Amy, whose younger sister Claire died of a tumour said of the group, 'It's not depressing. We talk over a cup of coffee and share feelings in various ways. Most friends don't understand what it's like. If I mention Claire they quickly change the subject.' Amy brought her friend Emma with her to SIBS first meeting. Emma used to visit when Clare was alive, she was there as the family lived through scan results, tests and treatment. Emma witnessed a great deal, 'Amy was very brave' she told me, 'We've been through loads of things together. I can tell if something is wrong and I'll help.'

But what does help? These bereaved children had many ideas. Amy thought it was much better not to try and forget what had happened as some people advised she should. Nor did she think it was a good idea to pretend her sister had never been alive. What helped her, she found, was talking about her sister. Also, her grandmother gathered lots of photographs of Claire and the family and displayed them in a large frame – there was no way this family were going to ignore Clare's life or death.

This flexibility and openness to all possible ways of helping a child to grieve is very important. In a study of adjustment to the death of a sibling what helped most was having knowledge of the diagnosis and the probable fatal outcome, helping in the care of the sick child, having the opportunity to say 'goodbye' near the time of death, attending the burial service or being with the family on the day of the funeral, being able to have some of the child's possessions, and having previously experienced the death of a relative or pet (Pettle and Lansdown 1986).

Sixteen-year-old Helen, whose brother Julian died, said, 'It's really hard when you lose the friendship of a brother. It's hard adapting to being an only child.' Additional pain may be felt by young people such as Helen if they believe that the dead brother or sister was the one who was most loved. This impression may well reflect the reality of the situation where the death was anticipated. In all probability the sick child will have taken up the majority of time and attention at the expense of other siblings. Where the dying child has been nursed in hospital, one parent is virtually resident there, which divides the family just as their need for each other is greatest.

Lots of reassurance is required to convince surviving children that they are wanted and loved and not merely 'second best'. A toddler whose sibling dies may interpret their mother's preoccupation with grief as a rejection of themself, and become difficult and demanding. They may feel lost and actually wander off and become lost, another example of an outward manifestation of inner distress.

Despite aphorisms to the contrary, children are affected by the death of a new born brother or sister, just as they are by late miscarriages or stillbirths. The following account, taken from the family's special album, makes that abundantly clear:

The Photo Album

Here is a photograph album dedicated to Thomas Matthew Williams. He was the second child born to Andrea and John Williams and the first brother or sister to me, Anna Williams, Andrea and John's first child. He was born on 29th July 1984 and died on February 6th 1985. He died at the Brompton Hospital in London. He was under anaesthetic so it was not a painful death. His funeral was at Southgate Church Centre on St. Valentine's Day 1985. He was about six months old when he died but at least he lived to see Christmas. I was in the second year at primary school and I was five years old.

We knew from the day he was born that there was a possibility of him dying and he used to be quite tired and have blue fits, but he was quite cheerful considering. What happened was that my Nana Williams was at our house looking after me while my Mum and Dad were at the hospital waiting in the ward, a hospital flat, or the intensive care unit. Mum had to say goodbye to him at the lift before he went into the operating theatre. There were two holes in his heart but the surgeons only knew about one, and when the operated they put too much strain on him and he died.

We had him cremated and planted a tree on Hardwick Heath in memory of him and scattered his ashes around the bottom. Then two and three quarter years ago Mum had Marcus and he brought great happiness to our family. I took a note around the close with all the details on it and could hardly wait to get away from school for visiting time at the hospital.

Mum and Dad, in 1985, had come home to tell me the news about Thomas on the 3.00am milk train from King's Cross Station. They did not want to phone because they wanted to be there to comfort me. They came in holding hands and crying. I knew straight away what had happened and leapt into their arms and bawled my eyes out.

The next few months especially were very painful. I had to have a few days off school around the time of his actual death and the funeral to get over the stress of it all. I used to cry a lot and feel uneasy when his name was mentioned but I have learnt to cope with it. Once a lady who did not know that Thomas had died asked Mum how he was and Mum burst out crying and walked away. Dad had to explain.

The doctors at Brompton Hospital will at least be able to help other children with the same problem as Thomas now.

Anna Williams

Anna's brother died when she was five. After his death the family prepared a photograph album with pictures of Thomas at birth, through his six months of life and some of him after his death, both on his own and in the arms of his mother and father. Photographs of his funeral and the tree planting ceremony also have their place. The last photograph is of Anna with her 'new' brother Marcus. Anna wrote her eloquent piece five years after Thomas's death when she was ten years old.

What happens when an older child loses a sibling? The response of the parents has an enormous influence and the child takes his or her cue from them. Rosemary, whom I quoted earlier, gave a personal account which reveals the depths of desolation such separation can induce.

I am a sixteen-year-old and have lost a brother. People say, 'Oh, it was only your brother', or even 'She doesn't understand, she was too young.' I was ten then. I had never known what it would be like not to have my brother Gerald, then one day I turned round and my Dad said, 'Rosemary, Gerald is going to die'. I didn't cry because I didn't believe him.

Then I saw my brother on a life support machine. He looked just like a battered doll. He was knocked down on his way from school. He was three years older than me. I was so upset but then I heard my brother's voice say, 'Don't cry!'

I just fought back the anger and the pain. I just helped my Mum and Dad through it. They didn't seem to notice how I was feeling but five years have gone by now and I am still angry, confused and sad. I can't talk about this to anyone because if I say anything to Mum I'll upset her and the same with Dad. I am so angry and sad.

Over the last five years I have dug myself into a pit and I can't get out. I just get deeper and deeper. I am frightened because I just can't see any way out. Not a day goes by when I don't think of what we did together. I just don't know what to do.

I once told this to my teacher shortly after Gerald's death. She said to just try to forget about it but I don't want to forget about Gerald, ever! But I get low and depressed at times, I just feel like ending it all and going to Gerald. But, I know I can't do that because Gerald will be mad with me, I'll upset Mum and Dad and I don't want to upset them. What can I do? Please give me some suggestions.

Rosemary

Rosemary's concise simplicity unequivocally communicates her pain. She could not express herself so forthrightly at home or at school, no adults in her world had been privy to her despair instead she wrote this letter in response to a radio programme about bereavement. Such helplines provide great succour for those isolated from support. How many other young people are in similar situations? Thankfully, Rosemary was offered counselling and finally came to terms with her loss. Her words reveal how lonely it can be when there is no one there to listen.

The process of grieving may take years, as it did for Rosemary. Somehow, the child finds a mode of operation that allows them to carry on daily life reasonably well, if somewhat under par, and those around forget that the impact of the loss still burdens them. The experience of an early loss of a sibling can be revived painfully at critical points later in life, such as when the child herself becomes a parent, during the early years of bringing up children, and when a child falls ill. The long term effects of loss last beyond the first anniversary, which we need to bear in mind as we counsel people in distress.

If we accept that this final reorganisation stage can be an ongoing process over many years, we will be sensitive to signs of stress and cries of help. One such signal may be the child's feelings of failure. The failure of their parents' marriage is seen by many children as a reflection of their own failure. They feel guilty because they had not made their parents' relationship better. They feel failures because they were not loveable enough, not worth the extra work that parents might have made to stay together. 'Surely', such a guilt-ridden child reasons, 'if I'd been good enough, my parents would have wanted to care for me, stay together and not cause all this misery?' After such a momentous failure, witnessed and endured, many of these children feel shocked and betrayed. Trust is one of the first fatalities in divorce.

Ann, now twenty, told me of the differing reaction in her family to her parents' divorce:

It was four years ago when my mother left. It came as no shock to me but my younger brother and sister were devastated. Then twelve years old, my sister's reponse was 'Was it my fault? Was it something I did?'

This hurt me more than my mother leaving. I was old enough to realise that the family was going to pull together, and in time be happier. The atmosphere had been shocking for years but looking back, after the initial shock and grieving by us all, we have ended up a closer and happier family.

My sister immediately turned to me as a mother figure and I took over the duties of running the house. This was a good situation for all of us until my sister started seeing her Mum again on a regular basis. She began to see her as a friend but still saw me as a mother figure. Therefore I was treated to all the moods and temper tantrums associated with adolescence. This is still very upsetting but I am hoping when I get married and get a house with my boyfriend, the relationship between my sister and myself will improve and maybe lead us to being very good friends.

I hope all of this has no lasting effect on her and does not colour her idea of marriage.

It is clear to see that this experience of loss directly affected Ann's life and increased her responsibilities in the family. She does not say how this influenced her educational choices but certainly she stayed at home, seeing her role as that of a substitute mother. There is just a hint of resentment in her comment that her sister was seeing '*her* mother' not '*our* mother', the distancing that followed the divorce is clearly visible in that pronoun.

What Ann's comments also highlight is the way in which children seek to allocate blame. In the midst of all the recriminations, and torn by divided loyalties, we have to help the child define divorce as the business of adults. They need to come to terms with their own powerlessness in changing the course of events and at the same time, when old enough, look after themselves during the changes inevitably going on around them.

Relief is a response easily overlooked when we consider reactions to loss, but it is worth remembering that one person's loss is another's gain. Not all children like their parents, let alone love them. For example, Nicola was glad when her parents finally got divorced. The strain had made her irritable and off-hand with her friends at school, which in turn caused outbursts there. Now aged fifteen, five years after that divorce, she says, 'Since they split up I've been much happier and I can control my temper.' Much of the anger she felt towards her father's drunken abuse has gone. Now she feels safe, she no longer needs to defend herself all the time. Divorce for Nicola meant she could relax.

Re-Structuring: Creating a New Family

No one believes that re-marriage and step-parenting – or its equivalent without the formality of marriage – is easy for anyone involved, especially the children. For many in the process of re-structuring their families, it is tempting to avoid the unpleasant facts that research presents. Yet, anyone who works with children needs to be aware of just how fraught life can be for families in transition.

Remarriage after divorce is taking a heavy educational, social and psychological toll on children (Kiernan 1991). They face more upheaval through the remarriage of a parent than when the parent stays alone, and the notion that children are resilient enough to survive divorce and remarriage without disadvantage is a myth. So why is it like this and what can you do to ease the strain?

Many children have to like it or lump it as far as many families are concerned. Parents and their new partners have got so much happening in their own lives that it is easy to overlook what is happening to the children, involved as they are with courtship, meeting new people, planning the future and sorting out housing. Children are involved, yet too often they are presented with a fait accompli – a 'new dad'. They may not have wanted any change in the first place and they may not be able to cope with the way in which their life is changing, even when the process appears to have been unhurried.

Jeff understood this when his partner and her two children moved in with him and his two children:

> Katherine was the most upset, she would say, 'I want to go back to 77, this is not my home'. I've let her grieve and I've tried to support her. It was not her choice and that's important to remember. We built it up gradually for them. The courtship was on the phone over three years, talking and taking things bit by bit to try to get over any fears they would have.

One reason a child cannot cope with the change is because she fears the new partner will take her parent(s) away from her. Such fear is perfectly natural and is self-protecting. Some children recognise these feelings and openly say they want the other person to 'go away', as does the girl in Anne Fine's brilliant book *Goggle Eyes* (Fine 1989). Another child may be more subtle or devious, behave badly, be more aggressive, moody, inconsistent and generally behave abominably.

Basically, a child feels insecure and needs lots of time, chance to talk, explanations and reassurances that they are still loved and that they will not be abandoned. The parent(s) can ease this by ensuring that they have special time with their child that is for them alone and which shows they are valued as an individual. We all need to feel we are special to someone and children recovering from divorce need this more than ever.

Step-parents are seen as the villains in the divorce drama, often blamed for causing the break-up, so they start off with a considerable handicap. If the new partner moves in too quickly without adequate preparation, then the children will quite rightly feel left out and disregarded. The anger that is felt towards the parent may be displaced onto the interloper, as John describes:

I couldn't tell my Mum that I hated her for bringing him to live with us, because she might leave us like Dad did. At least when she was there I knew someone would take care of us.

Natural justice comes into play too and many changes strike children as unfair, caught up as they are in messy adult relationships. Eleven-year-old Becky told me, 'I think it is unjust that I now see my Mum and Step-dad so much more than my real Dad.' Darren, aged twelve, certainly had no say in what happened to him after he was left in the care of his father following his parents' divorce when he was three. His first step-mother made a strong impression: 'When I had an accident, and her girls' head went through the door window, my step-mum smacked me and dragged me round the room by my hair.' That relationship did not become permanent: 'I had two step-mums that hated me, but in 1988 my Dad met someone who is really nice.' At last a happy ending but broken dreams, physical punishment and rejection along the way, which made his family transition very traumatic.

Children do feel put out by the new resident partner. They feel as though they are intruding having to knock on the bedroom door where previously they would have just walked in, and are jealous of this new intimacy that excludes them. However it can work out well given time and care. Alan liked the cosiness of being with his mother and his nine-year-old brother after his mother and father split up. He thought his mother worked very hard and he would have liked more time with her, but when she got a boyfriend he became anxious:

I wondered what he would be like. And half of me wanted to like him and half of me wanted him not to be there. And when my Mum said she was going to bring him home I was scared. He turned out to be tall and I was nervous and shy so I didn't say much. I still felt half and half but then I got used to him and I really like him now.

It was only after Alan got to know his would-be step-father that he felt relaxed enough to let down his guard. This period of adjustment is vital and should not be rushed. Many children need time to get over the trauma as Alex, now sixteen, recalled:

> My Mum and Dad split up when I was nine, but my Mum remarried when I was eleven. About that time and for a few years after, I had the same dream about when my Mum and Dad were arguing many times. My Mum would scream at my Dad and my Dad would begin to hit my Mum as I stood on the stairs. Now, I almost hate my Dad and call my Step-dad 'Dad'.

When parenting partners split up, children typically go through the grieving stages of denial, sadness, anger, guilt, depression, acceptance and renewed life spirit. They may be at any of these stages in the cycle when their parents establish new partnerships and so they will be differently affected according to which point they are at. Their feelings and behaviour will reflect this, as will their adjustment to the new union.

There are at least seven critical issues that the child has to deal with at such a time: They have to deal with loss, divided loyalties, decide where they fit in, get used to belonging to two households (or more), deal with unreasonable expectations, deal with his fantasies about his natural parents, and guilt about causing the divorce and /or causing upset in this new relationship. And then there is the whole issue of the extended step-family – new brothers and sisters. It is of paramount importance that time, sensitivity and empathy are to the forefront in resolving these difficulties. One boy speaking of his experiences said tellingly, 'My sister was like a piece of the family that didn't change'. Their relationship became closer and they remain solidly supportive of each other, each a firm anchor for the other in the sea of change.

Some children feel scared about telling other people that their mother or father is to re-marry. People might make comments or ask questions that embarrass the child. Most children hate to feel the odd one out and schoolmates can be insensitive. Alan said: 'Other children at school made fun of me. Two other boys in my class had step-dads and they didn't like theirs, so I was a bit worried that I wouldn't like mine'.

On re-marriage the child may be concerned that the other natural parent is being left behind or left out, or that the re-marrying parent has got one up on the other parent. The messages that the parents give to the children will influence this. Children will also feel very annoyed and left out if they are not told of wedding plans or not invited to the wedding. They might not go and indeed the parent who is not the one marrying might prefer their offspring not to attend; but children need to be given the choice to take part in these rites of passage – taking part in the ritual is important. If they are not offered the choice resentment may fester to ruin future relationships within this new 'blended' family.

Choice needs also to be offered about changing names. If the child's mother, for example, takes on the name of her new partner, the child may feel isolated and rejected, especially if there are step-siblings with the new name. He may feel disloyal if he changes his name since he believes that by doing so he is rejecting his father. This also has implications for school. His peers may make fun and his identity will be changed if he takes on a new name, so his views need to be taken into consideration.

There is another issue involving names: what does the child call the new step-parent? There must be choice here too. Back to Alan who had this problem when his new step-father finally joined the household. He explained to me, 'I already have my Dad so I didn't want to call Tom that, and Tom said that was OK. He said 'Why don't you just call me Tom?" Both are happy with that and Alan has no feelings of disloyalty to his father.

Strain is eased where consideration of the children involved is constant, not just in the 'honeymoon' weeks but consistently thereafter. If the new partner is heavy handedly trying to impose a completely different regime, without recognising that the child and parent had their own routines prior to their arrival, they will be bitterly rejected. Children hate the presumption the new adult thinks they can take over the role of the previous parent, as John revealed: 'What I really resented was that he thought he could tell me what to do. He had no right to tell me how to behave or to touch me. Who did he think he was?' In remembering his early days with his stepfather he admitted going out of his way to make life difficult. It was a way at getting back at them for making his life miserable: after all he had not wanted the divorce. He was helpless to do anything more than hang around all the time so that his Mum could not be with her new man on her own. He demanded her time and attention, tried to cause trouble by talking about the way his Dad did things (better of course!) and managed to feel he had some power, though he admitted he felt rotten about it all too.

To feel such helplessness causes severe strain for some children who understandably need to feel to some control over their own destiny. It feels better to do something bad than to do nothing at all. Action asserts the fact that you are there and demands some attention. It gives children hope, for whilst the parent can opt out of the situation, the offspring are rarely given the choice.

Being a good enough parent is a difficult and demanding job as any parent – or child for that matter – can tell you. It is especially so when a child is suffering and the parent is torn between conflicting loyalties to partners, ex-partners, children and the extended family. Throughout the period of transition the child needs the opportunity to express their views, to be listened to, to have a stable person who will offer unconditional love, and the opportunity to maintain relationships with both parents and step-parents, if they so wish. Otherwise a continued feeling of loss will dominate their life and result in increased stress. If this is so sleep patterns and dreams may be significantly affected, and it is to those that we now turn.

CHAPTER 5

Dreams as Distress Signals

'I'm walking along in a graveyard when I suddenly see my grave in the distance. I'm shocked that I'm there and I'm not sure what to do and my Mum and Dad have already died and I can see their graves as well. I just don't know what to do and it becomes a nightmare. I just, well, I just feel my life's falling apart because I don't know what to do.'

Moira (15)

Dreams are some of the most significant indicators of stress in a child's life. However, few families regularly exchange views about their dreams, few seek meanings as to why certain dreams happen at certain times. No one asked Moira, the girl whose dream is quoted at the beginning of this chapter, about her dream yet plainly it was very distressing. This recurring dream is one Moira has had for some time. She is managing well at school but keeps her feelings of stress well away from public display. When we spoke about her dream, she told me, 'I cry a lot because I don't know what it will be like when my Mum and Dad die, I don't know what it's going to be like without them. It's just something that worries me.'

Like so many children I work with, she has not spoken with anyone about her anxiety. She does not speak of her dream because she believes her parents would say she is being stupid. Alone, she grapples with the idea of separation and mortality: part of her is miserable as well as frightened, yet no one sees beyond her mask of confidence. As she is doing well at school they infer everything else is fine.

Children's dreams reflect the emotional turmoil of their waking life (see my book *Children Dreaming* for fuller details of the results of such research (Mallon 1989). This was certainly the case for six-year-old Liam. Two weeks before I met him, Liam had a severe shock. His father, whom he adored, left home. Since then Liam has been plagued by nightmares generally featuring his mother. In one he sprinkled magic dust on her and she shrank until eventually she was impaled on a stud of his football boot. In another he saw his mother hanging on a cross, crucified. When he looked up at her wounded body on that Easter cross he cried and cried.

Liam told me he had not cried when he was awake but he often wakes to find his pillow soaking. I asked him what made it hard for him to cry during the day if he was so upset, and he replied sadly that his mother would not like it and might be cross with him. He knew his mother was upset about his father leaving but talking about it was 'not allowed'. The imagery of the dream shows the ultimate public 'crucifying' of his mother, whilst he, an onlooker, can only powerlessly stand by and witness the tragedy. His dreams reflect a changing relationship where everything is out of proportion and in a state of flux.

At school, where Liam felt safe and happy, there were no overt signs of anguish, but the dreams expressed his deep loss, anger with his mother for not preventing his father's departure, and terror, unspoken until that afternoon, that something would happen to his mother and she too would change and abandon him. For the first time he expressed his fear that his mother might leave him too.

He was relieved to hear that many other children whose parents separate have similar worries and distressing dreams. Using his dreams as the starting point I was able to assure him that his mother was not going to leave, and helped him identify other members of his extended family who could care for him. But can separation be anything other than difficult for a child like Liam, unless of course there is unrelenting abuse within the family? Certainly conflict puts a strain on the child, which then shows up in dreams.

Prior to any talk of separation, Kelly's dreams showed that she knew something was going wrong. In one dream she told me, she went to the fair with her mother and father, but then, 'My Mum and Dad had an argument and my Mum walked away and they had a divorce.' Her dreams reflect their divide and reveal the intuitive awareness that many children have about events within the family that have not been revealed. It prepared Kelly for one possible outcome but she was in a 'Catch 22' situation. Her parents had not told her of any impending separation so she was afraid of revealing, by telling her dream, that she knew more than she was supposed to know, so she kept quiet.

Rachel was surprised when similar news was broken to her: 'One day my Mum sat me down in the lounge and told me that her and my Dad were going to split. I dreamt nothing about it for ages and then, all of a sudden, I kept having these really horrible dreams about it. I wasn't worried about them splitting up but I didn't like the dreams.' The anxiety Rachel had about the separation surfaced in her distressing dreams. Six months later, I asked her if the dreams had stopped. 'Yes,' she replied, 'because we're living in a house on our own now so it's really quite peaceful. I suppose I was worried and it just played on my mind really.' At the time of the separation she was determined not to think about it and avoided any discussions. All she wanted was for it to be over and done with, so she could get on with her life in peace.

Violent dreams like Liam's or like five-year-old Susie's in which she brutally kills birds and other small creatures, are not uncommon following a separation. Sometimes they mirror what the child feels has been done to them, whilst for others they reveal disguised anger about the situation. Such cathartic dreams provide a safe way for the child to discharge those feelings of destruction, to get back at others, without getting punished or risking further loss. However, these disturbing feelings may permeate waking moods and leave children feeling ill at ease.

Themes of being chased or trapped are prevalent in children who feel vulnerable. This one of twelve-year-old Jilly is typical:

> I dream of being chased and I cannot run fast enough. I dream of being pushed off a cliff and just keep falling. My parents argue a lot and that upsets me and because I am worrying, I am grumpy and miserable. My friends are fed up with me and are not speaking to me.

The increase in her disturbing dreams exactly mirrors the build up of pressure at home as her parents' marriage disintegrates, and she easily made the connection once she had the opportunity to talk confidentially.

Nine-year-old Jennifer also had falling dreams like Jilly's except that her mother and sister as well as herself were being pushed over the edge of a cliff, just as in waking life she felt as if she was being pushed 'over the edge'. There was no protective boundary to keep her safe. There was no safe ground left in her family for, as she explained, 'It's hard with my family falling apart. Now my Dad's gone and one of the best parts of my family, my Nan, has died.' The dream reveals a lack of solid support, no protection and the impact of sheer uncertainly when the ground is no longer beneath your feet.

Experiencing deeply disturbing dreams night after night can lead to feelings of deep fatigue, possibly to the point of depression. One fourteen-year-old boy painted a powerful illustration of a dream he had had repeatedly, five times a week, two years before I met him. In it a naked body lay face down at the bottom of a flight of stairs, sprawled out as if dead. Jonathan, a serious, quiet boy from Belfast stuttered a little as he spoke about it:

> In my dream I would be lying in bed thinking about something then I would just get up and walk out. I couldn't stop myself from walking and I would stand on the landing for two or three minutes and I would just jump

off and I would float down. I would be trying to stop but it just felt like a force was pulling me down or something, some pressure.

Jonathan gazed at the vulnerable figure he had painted so beautifully, and recalled how he would wake up in a cold sweat afraid to go back to sleep in case it came back.

He connected the pressure he felt in the tormenting dream to the problems in his life at that time. He had never made the link before. He described his dream:

> The dream is in the room where my mother and father were. They were fighting a lot and there was one time when, see, my father had too much to drink and he came in from the bar one time and him and my Mum were arguing. I think my father was going to strike my Mum, and I – I ran down the stairs and the last couple of steps actually fell and I bumped into him as he was raising his hand.

He told me that he almost felt a pull to bring him downstairs that night. 'It was about three o'clock in the morning and usually I'm a good sleeper but that night, the night it happened, I was restless.'

Maybe he was worried too about the way his parents were treating each other, maybe woken by the early stages of an argument or sleeping lightly in anticipation of a violent disagreement. Whatever the reason Jonathan's dream was repeated night after night for over two years after that night, until he came to terms with the trauma and until his parents resolved some of their problems.

I asked Jonathan why he had not spoken with anyone about the dream.

> There was no one to talk to. You see, my dad, if you talk to him about anything he's not a serious person, he starts laughing at me...I just wish someone had talked it over with me and reassured me that it was all right. But it wasn't all right at the time, you see my mother and my two sisters were moving out and leaving but then we all moved back together and the dream just stopped.

So not only had he suffered the terror of unwittingly intervening in his parents quarrel, he had been left behind when his mother and sisters left home. As he was older, more capable, he had to stay with a man who clearly ridiculed his thoughtful, introspective son. The dreams were at their height during that period of desertion and they readily portray both the pressures on John and his symbolic destruction. Part of John did die when his mother left him to fend for himself with a violent man she herself did not trust. It was the end of John's childhood. If only there had been someone to turn to, to ease the pain of those years.

Thirteen-year-old Sally, whose parents recently divorced, dreams of her father sitting alone in an empty house. She understands that the dreams show her waking concern for her father but another dream in which both her parents are dying causes her real distress. After that recurring dream she finds it impossible to go back to sleep. When I explained to Sally that dreams of death usually indicate that some aspect of life has ended, she was relieved. Realising that it did not really mean her parents were literally going to die she understood that it was her parents' life together, their marriage, that had 'died'.

Terrifying dreams extend into waking life so that some children actually become afraid of letting go of the day. For these children there is no escape in sleep until their waking anxiety is resolved. Jean, an adult client with whom I worked, was sexually abused by her father over a period of years. The abuse extended to other members of her family and her mother offered no protection. Regularly Jean dreamt that she and her brother killed her parents so that they could go and live with their grandparents. 'But' she said, 'we always used to push a car, which wasn't really our car, over a cliff'. I always woke up crying with my face and hair wet.' In the dream the car is destroyed but her parents are not.

A child who has suffered extreme trauma is likely to experience nightmares and recurring threat in their dreams. Most children who have been sexually abused subsequently suffer from recurrent nightmares of being chased, attacked and killed (Maisch 1973). Indeed some experts say that in older children the first overt sign of sexual abuse is sexually explicit acting out behaviour, whilst nightmares are the next. One survivor, Barbara Myers, in an open letter to her father, described the ordeal and its legacy:

> You destroyed my ability to sleep, to think, to develop. My nights were horrors. I used to lie awake in bed and worry whether you were going to come in my room. Sometimes the night fears would overtake me and I would dream – or perhaps hallucinate – evil things happening. Sometimes you would take me from my room and tell me I had sleepwalked. You destroyed my trust in my own sanity.

One reason for these traumatic dreams is that the child unconsciously seeks to make sense of their painful experience. They continue to process the event as they sleep. A child's dreams act as a barometer of emotional well-being, they communicate the level of the child's stress and give insight into unconscious turmoil. Frequently distressing dreams reveal the crippling burden of disturbed family relationships.

Tina, now married with children of her own, described her early dreams:

> Throughout my childhood, between the ages of eight and thirteen, I had recurring dreams. In one I am walking down a road supporting my mother who can't walk without me. Suddenly a black witch comes out of a house screaming 'Go back! Go home!'. Apart from the fright I realise that I have to get back home with Mum as quickly as possible or something will happen. On the corner of a street is a huge castle with winding, shadowy corridors. It is taking us longer and longer and Mum is getting heavier and heavier. We finally reach our gate to see my father, Nana and others holding out their arms and wailing 'Too late! Too late!' then they hazily disappear into the house. I know they are ghosts and know I am too late.

Other dreams were equally burdensome and in none were offers of assistance made. She was always solely responsible for her own survival. Tina explained her family circumstances which revealed the original impetus for these dreams. Her mother had tuberculosis and extensive surgery before marrying. The doctors advised her not to have children but she gave birth to a boy, then Tina three years later. Her father was an alcoholic, inadequate but 'charming and inoffensive'. Tina felt her mother stayed alive for her children especially after Tina's father left when she was eight. 'My contact with him was always superficial compared with the intensity of my relationship with my mother', Tina said, 'She had strength and humour but I always felt responsible if she were in pain or depressed.'

Tina's childhood was dominated by feelings of responsibility for her mother's welfare, the traditional role of parent/caregiver was imposed on her at a very early age. Although Tina was sociable and successful at school, able and intelligent, she felt that her childhood ended prematurely. Her dreams reflect her feelings of abandonment by her extended family too, a theme reflected in many children's dreams.

Children sometimes deliberately conceal concerns about distressing dreams, as eight-year-old Diane did:

> I once dreamt that my mother was screaming for me and coming upstairs with a leather belt to beat me. I could hear her screaming and her footsteps on the stairs getting closer and closer. I was terrified. When I awoke I nearly told her about it but was really afraid of her and thought she would hurt me if I told her the truth.

Dreams allow the child to recognise the dual nature of people, the 'good' caring part and the not-so-good powerfully threatening part. Ten-year-old Kelly has recurring dreams about a man dragging her out of bed, attempting to kill her. Though that is disturbing enough, there is an even more traumatic recurring dream, as she told me: 'The most frightening dream I have is of my Daddy turning into a mean man who kills all my friends and I know it was him. He said to me if I were to tell anyone that it was him he would kill me and my Mammy.' Abusers, as Kelly's father was, threaten children into secrecy by saying they will injure or kill either the child or a non-involved parent or sibling (Miller 1991). The fear induced almost invariably forces a child to remain silent, but dream voices do not allow the threat to go unvoiced. Another girl Pattie, aged twelve, was reduced to tears when she dreamt that her 'real father', a violent, abusive man, came back to take her away from her well-loved step-father. Luckily, she did tell her family. They listened to the dream narrative and offered the reassurance Pattie still needed.

As you can see, family relationships figure prominently in stress dreams, and give plenty of clues as to a child's pre-occupations and anxieties. Colette provided a good example: 'I was awful to my brother one night and my Mummy said to me "If ever anything happened to him now, how would you feel?" Then that night I had an awful dream that he died and I woke up the next day crying. It was terrible.' When she woke up Colette believed her brother had really died and rushed to his room. She was so relieved to find he was still alive that she was determined to be much nicer to him. 'Was he pleased?' I asked her. 'No, not really. He was too shocked!' she replied.

Not all distressing dreams are directly about separation, some dreams are very much influenced by illness for instance, but there are still hints of separation anxiety as the following children show. Renee recalled that between the ages of eight and ten she repeatedly dreamt that 'they' – 'and I haven't a clue who "they" were' – were going to turn her tummy upside down. She said, 'I would wake up absolutely terrified, crying and calling out for my mother. It took her ages to calm me down and convince me that I was safe.' Renee actually feared going to sleep in case the dream returned. 'Recently', she continued, 'I realised that this dream was about my own childhood trauma. I fractured my femur when I was two years and nine months and had to spend six weeks in hospital in traction, and I was not allowed to see my family at all during this time. I have no conscious memory of this experience. I only discovered it when I was about nine and saw a film in which a man was in traction, and I was terrified as soon as I saw it! 'My "tummy turning upside down" was my childish way of interpreting what had happened to scare me so much.' It is not unusual for repressed traumatic events to be first glimpsed in dreams before they fully enter conscious thoughts.

Fevers cause vivid dream imagery for some children. 'At the age of nine', recalled Simon, 'I had chicken pox. I can still remember the nightmare of London burning and people madly trying to get in boats on the Thames.' High temperatures often induce this kind of burning imagery as eight-year-old Nicola discovered. She dreamt that her body was being burned while she was still alive, a waking cremation. Though she tries to 'get out' in her dream, the only way she can escape is by waking up. The content of Emily's dream is different though still distressing:

> When I am feverish I always have the same dream, in which everything is very distorted and somehow larger than it should be. When I was very little I used to dream about a mute swan and I remember feeling scared because, like the swan, I couldn't call out.

This sensation of being paralysed, dumb and powerless is shared by many caught in stressful situations, and illness does cause great strain in children, as you will see in the next chapter. However, another dream that reflects this type of stress is one of eleven-year-old Jessica's, who not only found herself mute during her recurring bouts of tonsillitis, but something more:

> When I was ill with my throat, I dreamt that I was going to swallow my tonsils and choke on them. Then I dreamt I was going to die because I had nothing to drink and I was choking. My face went blue and I died.

The symptoms of the illness echo in her dreams. It is useful to remind ourselves of this fear factor when we come across children who are ill, either in medical settings or in care situations. Though we take recovery for granted, children may not.

A recurring dream of Tessa's, now thirteen, was very disturbing:

> Every time I had the problem, I had the dream. I was in a white place, just totally white – that was the first part. Then I was being chased by sheep, gaining on me all the time, then I went into this other place. It was black. And the blackness was coming closer and closer and I could not get away from it. Suddenly there were all these sort of black ribbons. And they were spouting more ribbons and more. They were slowly getting thicker and thicker covering all around me. I couldn't get out of it but then I went into another room. There was a big mangle in it that I was drawn into. It was going round and round with me going through it. Never-ending, on and on. Finally, I came out the other end and I was OK. I wasn't squashed or anything, but then a big black ball would chase me and was just covering me, and then I usually woke up or my Mum woke me up because she said I was crying in my sleep. I'd be covered in sweat.

This unusual dream with its distinct sections happened when Tessa began to go into liver failure. She has not had the dream for over a year now, ever since her liver disease was treated successfully, though it had caused ill-health since she was five years old. Her 'through the mangle' dream reflected her feeling of being 'wrung out, like a wet rag', completely depleted. Now, clear of the threat of impending life-threatening attacks, her dreams are free of this kind of chase/attack/being engulfed imagery.

Illness and disability heighten feelings of vulnerability, which shows in dream imagery as we can see in thirteen-year-old Robert's dream: 'When I am ill', he said, 'I dream that I have got the Black Plague and nobody will go near me.' Other children dream of quarrels with friends, of being bullied or being ostracised as was twelve-year-old Lee. He dreamt that all of his friends turned traitor on him, ganged up, and, he said, 'Duffed me up so badly that everyone thought I was dead.' But he was revived in hospital and a disguise made to protect him in future. At the conclusion of the dream he lived with his doctor–saviour and took revenge on all his 'friends', one at a time. Revenge was sweet as he lived under the care of the archetypal life-saver, the doctor. The need for a new identity is interesting and may reflect the transition taking place during adolescence. Many young people feel the need to disguise their true attitudes or feelings because of the profound need to have the approval and acceptance of the peer group.

Dream symbols represent aspects of the dreamer's life. Frank felt his family had no idea about what he liked, what bothered him; in other words he thought they were completely out of touch with him. One dream reflects this theme: 'The most frightening dream I have had was when I disappeared and found myself in an old castle where a man turned me invisible, and no-one could see me or hear me and I was all alone.' Frank's dream reveals his feelings of isolation by making him invisible. As no-one ever notices him in waking life, he subconsciously thinks he might as well be invisible. He has a nightmare in which he is at the top of the stairs and has to jump. At first his mother is waiting to catch him, urging him on, but when he jumps she disappears. There is no-one to save him, no-one there to help him when he is so dependent. This confirms his feeling of vulnerable isolation. People make promises to him in dreams, as they do in his waking world, but they break them. Frank feels unable to trust people and this is symbolised in his disturbing dreams.

Six weeks prior to attending her new secondary school, twelve-year-old Gillian dreamt of being chased, then of walking down the street only to find she had on nothing but a T-shirt. Everyone looked at her and pointed out her nakedness. She knew it was because she was fearful of the change: 'I was sort of worried because everyone used to keep me going, saying I'd get my head stuck down the toilet and I'd get beaten up. I thought the school would be really big and I'd never find my way about.' Gillian did not feel safe at the time, though she told no-one, but the dreams stopped once she settled into her new surroundings.

For children attending boarding school the change can be even more traumatic. The separation from family, home and familiar surrounding can be terrifying. Sad and frightening dreams abound, so sources of comfort have to be found, especially if like eight-year-old Eric you are afraid of the dark too. When I asked him what he did when one of his 'being chased' dreams woke him up, he replied, 'I usually wake Daniel, he's in the bunk above me, and then if he doesn't want to help, I ask Jeremy who is opposite. They comfort me and tell me stories to get my mind off my dream. Then when I'm feeling better I try and get back to sleep.'

Other boarders told me of distressing dreams and a few revealed a similar fear of the dark. Daniel, who had just moved to a new choir house, seemed ashamed as he admitted, 'I'm eleven and I've still got comforters, two bits of ribbon. At night I put them in my hands and then I sleep.' They helped somewhat but did not completely dispel the night monsters he said, 'But each night, it comes back, the same old fear.' Lots of the boys talk to each other in the dark as a way of combating those fears, whilst others surreptitiously cuddle babyhood soft toys, a link with safer times perhaps.

Rita described a recurring dream which started shortly after she went to boarding school for the first time:

> I'm walking down a path and suddenly I get separated from my Mum, my brother and my Dad. I'm separated by a stream and I keep trying to get towards my parents but something pulls me back everytime. My parents and my brother are all happy but I'm sad. It's all dull and gloomy around where I am but not where they are.

She started boarding when she was eight and felt the dream did reflect her earlier anxiety about the change. 'I did mind a bit about boarding at the beginning', she said, 'I'd moan and groan but I had to get used to it. I had no choice.' There were other problems as well: 'We used to live in South America until I was about seven, but then my Mum and Dad got divorced so we came over here back to Cambridge.' With so many stressful changes at once it is hardly surprising that Rita should feel isolated. No particular help was offered at the time, though she described it as a really terrible, upsetting period of her life.

Common sense tells us that this is likely to be the case, yet so often we choose to deny separation anxiety in children. When she told her mother about the dream and how upset she felt, her mother said, 'Don't worry, it will probably stop.' It did not stop for two years. Work with children in residential settings could afford the opportunity to discuss dreams and so help them resolve issues about separation and relationships.

Recurring dreams of falling happen at examination time for Stella. No matter how she tries she cannot prevent herself from tumbling down a never-ending hole. 'I try to grab onto the sides but I can't. I just can't get a grip.' Sometimes, Stella, who is very concerned that she achieves good academic results, feels she cannot 'get a grip' metaphorically speaking, on her work. Unpleasant dreams prior to examinations are not at all uncommon, and as well as using stress reduction techniques such as relaxation, young people can use the strategies at the end of this chapter to help them with their stressful dreams.

There is a special type of recurring, often literal nightmare that follows overwhelmingly intense and unexpected events. People suffering Post-traumatic Stress Disorder (PTSD) are likely to have these extremely disturbing dreams, and whilst we will look at PTSD in much greater detail in Chapter 7, here we are concerned about the effect of trauma on children's dreams.

Nightmares following trauma may continue for years, particularly at times when the dreamer is reminded of her past helplessness. Lenore Terr of the University of California School of Medicine studied a group of 26 children who had been kidnapped from their school bus in Chowchilla, California, and then buried alive by their three abductors (Terr 1987). They were held captive for almost 27 hours. Four to five years later many of the children, whose ages ranged from five to fourteen years, still had nightmares which exactly repeated the trauma and, in addition, many of the group tended to walk, talk or scream in their sleep.

As time passed the recurrent kidnapping dreams of the Chowchilla children became more elaborate so that in some cases the original trauma became hidden underneath layers of other dream material. Such disguised nightmares tell us that the children can suffer from PTSD for a long time after the trauma. Other children who have experienced psychologically overwhelming life events dream that they themselves die. Such personal death dreams often indicate that a traumatic event has indeed taken place in the past, and these children die in their dreams because they no longer believe in personal invulnerability.

Eleven-year-old Shaista told me of a dream she had repeatedly: 'I had to light fire to my house when everybody was asleep because two people came in and thought my Dad was a bank manager and they wanted to rob the bank...so they told me to light fire to my house, but I didn't and they lit fire to me.' Shaista becomes a human torch in her dreams. In her waking world a number of houses in her area have been subject to racist arson attacks. The waking trauma is translated in her dreams yet no-one knew how stressful this was for Shaista because she could not tell anyone. Talking about it was too frightening for this withdrawn little girl, who knew her whole family was worried too. In order to protect them, she kept silent. The nightmares though, reveal her unvocalised fears.

In dreams we try to find a way of making sense of seemingly senseless acts. There is evidence to show that the repetition in dreams of actual traumatic situations helps us to recover from the extreme experience of helplessness and powerlessness by re-living them until we find some way of resolving them. Children whose dreams go over the same theme again and again may benefit from strategies, discussed later in this chapter, which will help ease the sometimes crippling pain. But the first vital step you can take is to listen to the dreams the child tells and take them seriously.

David's dreams repeatedly featured death, and like Liam's were sparked off by a traumatic separation. He told me that his most frightening one involved a car crash in which every member of his family died except for him: 'Only I lived and was paralysed so I couldn't kill myself'. Such stark hopelessness is crying out for resolution and as we searched for explanations he described, as a contrast, his happiest dream: 'I went back into the past and changed everything that happened on the 5th of May because that was the day my younger brother was killed in a cycling accident.' David had to face the cruellest of blows: the sudden tragic death of his brother. He had no chance to prepare, no chance to say 'goodbye'. The stark reality of such a death frequently leaves the bereaved reeling. Their mourning may be more complicated and take much longer than in those where death was anticipated and more in the natural order. In David's dream he is paralysed, which symbolises his feeling of utter powerlessness in preventing his brother's death.

Horrendous nightmares also dominated bereaved Lily. In many, all her family were murdered or sickened and died, in others she was ill and the doctor gave her medicine which killed her. The dreams reduce the pale twelve-year-old to tears, but in the quiet of her empty classroom, it soon became apparent that Lily had many reasons to be distressed. Two of her brothers had died and her father and mother were divorced. She said, 'I don't think that my Dad leaving upset me, it's just when I see pictures of my brothers. I want to cry but I don't know what my Mum would say.' Lily was never encouraged to talk about her grief or work through the losses. Most of the time she managed to bury it under her daily activity, but when asleep the emotional distress would not stay repressed. As she is too frightened to talk to her mother for fear of being told off, it is a caring teacher who must recognise her anguish and then offer support, and possibly refer her on to a more specialised agency.

Obviously some children will need specialised treatment after a trauma, as Mark's story shows. Felice Cohen, an American art therapist, worked with Mark whose brother Scottie died in a fire inadvertently started by both boys (Cohen 1978). Mark was referred for therapy two years after the fire. At that time he had a range of problematic symptoms: he ate compulsively, hit and bit himself, and provoked fights with his friends and family and was increasingly out of control. He seemed constantly to seek out punishment and the situation in the family was becoming intolerable.

Mark's parents did not openly express their grief at their son's tragic death, and Mark was largely ignored, left unconsoled and not given any opportunity to express his sorrow. Obviously their own ambivalent feelings towards him were extremely difficult to cope with.

Cohen says that after four months of painting pictures Mark began to accompany his drawings with descriptions of his tormented dreams, in which red-hot fires consumed him. He asked why he had not been able to go to his brother's funeral, why his parents would not talk to him about Scottie, and asked why he too could not have died. That was the turning point in the therapy. No-one had ever explained what had happened to him, no-one had ever used the word 'accident' in reference to the tragedy. Stuck in his mind was the image that Scottie was taken away and no-one ever mentioned him again.

After a further three months of therapy, in which he came to terms with his pain, anger and hurt, and learned that he had not murdered his brother, Mark's presenting problems disappeared. The family was able to openly express their grief and share as a family once more. And Mark's nightmares stopped. His dreams offered the key to unlock his disturbed feelings so he could begin the journey to emotional recovery.

Dreams may also comfort the child who has suffered loss, as Thea's did: 'When I was about five and I was ill, I dreamt that an angel appeared in the room and my mother explained to her about my illness. She gave a blessing and I was instantly cured. In reality I was a little better next day.' Other wish-fulfilment dreams give children a sense of being united once again with a loved person: 'In reality my father died nearly six years ago of leukaemia. I dreamt not long ago that the doorbell went and he was standing on the doorstep with his case, ready to come home.' Justine felt positive about the dream and saw that whilst part of her deeply wanted her father alive and home again, in waking life she knew it was not possible. This dream was treasured because it gave her the chance to see him again.

Nine-year-old Paul also had his longing fulfilled in a dream:

In my dream all the family was at the crematorium. My Grandad had died. The coffin was just about to disappear behind the curtains and the vicar was just saying, 'Now Sidney G...is to be cremated.' Just then there was a croaking noise from the coffin. It started to open and Grandad got out of it. After that everything was alright.

Paul's mother explained the unusual circumstances surrounding this dream: 'On the third night after Grandad died, my husband too had a similar dream to Paul's. He dreamt that there was a knock on the door and a doctor appeared with my husband's father. He said they had taken Grandad to hospital and removed something from his throat, and he was now perfectly alright!' She continued, quite perplexed by these events, 'Both my husband and Paul rarely remember their dreams but this one stuck with them and each was able to recall it. Next day we talked about the dreams and Grandad's death at length.' Somehow the dreams gave an easy opportunity to talk about their feelings as a family.

The obvious wish-fulfilment in Paul's and his father's dreams, that somehow Grandad's death verdict had been a mistake, led to them sharing their thoughts and feelings in a healing way. At the end Paul was able to say, 'I know Grandad's happy in heaven with Granny, but I just wish he was here with us too.'

For other children dreaming is a way of recreating the good times. Twelve-year-old Stuart dreamt that his grandfather, who is dead, sat on the end of his bed and sang to him. The dream helped him to remember happy times with his grandfather and sustain the emotional link that was so important to him. Many bereaved people long for dreams of the person who has died and are reassured by them, as was Debbie. She dreamt that her grandmother told her she was happy and well and that the family need not be upset about her death anymore. For Debbie, it was permission to 'let go', permission to finish grieving and get on with her life without feeling guilt that she was letting her gran down by not being sad.

After Helena's grandmother died she came to a moment of revelation:

There was a big staircase from heaven and my granny came down on it and everyone came down behind her and there wasn't enough room for me and my mates and big things were rolling down towards us and we were all screaming. This big voice was saying 'Right, you're just going to have to die.'

She explained, 'My granny had just died and I imagined her coming down from heaven.' But then, for the first time, she faced the painful truth that death is permanent, 'I didn't realise that she couldn't come back down again.' Though aged twelve, Helena had never come in contact with death before, and its finality shocked her.

It is easy to disregard the loss of security children feel as they become aware of the world around them. War, famine, disasters, horrors and violence are the daily fare of our television and video diet. Children watch and are affected by it, perhaps brutalised by it, and it influences their dreams. Thirteen-year-old Brian has never been near an explosion but he has seen them on the news and now he dreams of them: 'There were flashing lights outside my window and when I looked out people were running everywhere. Explosions and gunshots everywhere. People were getting killed all over the place and when I looked closer I saw myself down there running around and hiding.'

Children in Northern Ireland have much more of this kind of imagery in their dreams than other children in Great Britain and they have more nightmares about war and death. Tracey, now eleven, from the Ardoyne district of Belfast, dreamt of military and para-military groups, like so many children in the province: 'I dreamt about a man who was a member of a force in the army, who got blew up right in front of my eyes. Then I got shot three times in the eyes so I couldn't identify the person who blew the soldier up.' As an innocent witness she is still not safe. The daily stress of living in a war torn environment takes a heavy toll of children, though too often we manage to avoid thinking about it.

Josie, a fourteen-year-old high school pupil, like most of her peers has dreams in which the conflict features. 'With the troubles in Northern Ireland, the way there's lots of fighting between Protestants and Catholics,' she explained, 'our dreams are a reflection about how we feel. Like if there has just been a bombing and you've been listening to it on the news, it sometimes comes in your dreams, where it happens to you. I get dreams sometimes where I'm locked in a room because the troubles are so bad I can't go out. I'm just locked in the one room the whole time.'

As for so many of her generation, she was trapped by the troubles. Her parents tried as far as possible to keep her safe indoors, away from any unexpected violence. Nicola, also fourteen, dreams of hands floating around her, coming closer and closer as if to strangle her. She regularly screams out and her mother comes in to comfort her. 'In the dream voices say 'We're coming to get you. We're going to get you,' she explained. 'I don't know why exactly I have these dreams but its probably because of all the shooting. It just gets into your mind and sometimes I'm afraid to go out. I think I'm going to get shot at or something like that.' There is not much talk about the impact of the 'troubles' at home, other than to comment on the most recent outbursts, but the turmoil batters the emotions of these children whether they speak of it or not.

Of course, the daily army presence prior to the first peace agreement, circling helicopters, army patrol cars that were ever-visible on the roads, as well as military activity, could not but impinge upon the conscious and unconscious world of all caught in the horrendous situation. As another girl told me when I worked with a group of pupils at a Belfast school, 'It's hard not to be affected because it's part of our lives. We live with it every day. Bombs going off round the corner and guns going off in the middle of the night. It's just part of our life. You live with it, you grow up with it.' Another girl reported a dream she had: 'One night I had this dream about being shot and it was really painful. I remember the pain all night in my leg and the next day I woke up and there was a big red mark on my leg.' The mark was caused by an audio cassette box which had accidently been left under her duvet. The external physical stimulus for the pain was obvious but notice how it is associated with the daily preoccupations of living in the midst of the civil war at that time.

She has other distressing dreams, and nervously biting her lip she expanded on their origin:

Sometimes I'm just lying in bed and I think to myself what it is like for those people on television that are getting shot, what it would be like getting killed. I just lie and think of what way would be easier and then I dream about it. Say I dream of myself being stabbed or hung or shot. Then I get up the next morning, I remember it all and I say to myself, that was awful. I'd rather be shot than stabbed because I think it would be easier. Once you're shot that's it.

Her fourteen years weighed heavy on her shoulders as she pondered the least painful form of death. 'You're frightened of the troubles coming closer to your house, you could be next. It's just frightening.'

Eileen was twelve when she was evacuated from London to a farm in Wiltshire. She got on so well with her substitute parents that eventually she did not want to go back home. The conflict caused by that was translated into recurring dreams over a two-year period. They featured two armies which converged on her and, although she wanted to run, she was rooted to the spot and she couldn't escape. Her powerlessness in these 'wars' – World War II which sent her away and the 'war' of her feelings about her old home and new billet – left her trapped. Children frequently have dreams in which they are trapped or paralysed and it is useful to ask what this mirrors in their waking life.

At times of loss dreams can be particularly disturbing as we have already seen. John Bowlby reported that about one-fifth of grieving children experienced acute night terrors, whilst a quarter insisted on sleeping with a parent or sibling at night (Bowlby 1980). If you inform children that this may happen after a trauma, they will be less taken by surprise. Obviously you don't tell them 'You *will* have nightmares' but gently explain that it sometimes happens. Dreams can be the vehicle for fears to be expressed. I have met children who thought they must be going mad because of their 'strange' dreams, so reassurance is of paramount importance. Directly acknowledging that the child is in a tense situation and explaining that their dreams are a safety valve which let off some of the pressure, often eases some of the anxiety about bad dreams.

In the normal busy world in which we live, where most activities are played out against a backdrop of incessant noise, many children have no quiet time or space to consider the wide variety of their experiences. Where a traumatic event has occurred it is important that the child has the opportunity to quietly 'do nothing'. Thinking, day dreaming and night dreaming are all part of coming to terms with the trauma.

A word here about sleepwalking. Though not directly related to dreaming it is related to stress. Sleepwalking, or somnambulism, is not an acting out of dreams but the confused and anxious thoughts of deep sleep; and it peaks in adolescence. Research indicates that it runs in families but the trigger is usually anxiety. The sleepwalker rises from bed, unaware of the world around them, unresponsive to attempts to attract their attention, and moves about, perhaps searching through drawers or cupboards. Next day they recall nothing of these happenings which may last from fifteen to thirty minutes, and may well not believe it when told. A sleepwalker should not be woken but guided back to bed. Usually sleepwalkers stop as suddenly as they start, but doors to the outside should be kept locked, though a child's bedroom door should not. After the child has rambled they usually make their own way back to bed, unharmed and unaware, to continue with their sleep.

Another disturbing sleep phenomenon is night terrors, *pavor nocturnus*. These are not nightmares but a sudden horrifying sensation which shocks the sleeper into wakefulness. The images terrify the child who commonly sits bolt upright, gazing at whatever imagined being is there, and screams or addresses the object. Such a child is awake but extremely confused and may be completely unresponsive to words of consolation or explanation that they are safe. The child may need lengthy reassurance before they settles back to sleep. Stressful as this is for the adult witness at the time, the child has no memory of the event in the morning and rarely suffers ill effects. Recent treatments of chronic sufferers of this sleep disorder have been most rewarding and can be tried at home. The treatment, spread over over a few nights, involves monitoring the time that the night terrors start, then on subsequent nights the child is gently woken about fifteen minutes prior to the expected terror. They should then be kept awake for about five minutes, maybe with a drink or soothing talk, then settled back to sleep. Three or four nights of this should be all that is needed to rid the child of their night terrors.

When faced with a dream-distressed child as opposed to the sleep-disordered child, there are some simple strategies that can be used. Parents may be helped if you provide the following list:

Strategies to Help Children Understand and Manage Their Dreams

1. Create a caring atmosphere

Try to maintain a caring, accepting, non-judgemental atmosphere in which the child feels safe to talk. Dreams are not 'good/bad' or 'right/wrong', so never tell a child they are bad because of their dreams. Do not be cross with a child whose dreams are upsetting you. Do not trivialise them, they are an important means of communication. Empathise and show you recognise the feelings the dream has evoked.

2. Listen

Listen to what the child says and ask open questions which enable them to tell his story in their own way. Encourage them to explore the dream, for instance you could ask, 'How did you feel in the dream?', 'Did you find anyone to help you out?', or 'What was the best/worst bit of your dream?' By listening you show the child that you value what they have to say and this increases the child's self esteem and belief in you.

3. Respect confidentiality

A child needs trust. They need confidentiality and to feel that they are a respected individual. If they choose to talk to you about their dreams that is fine, but do not abuse that trust by talking to others about their dreams without getting their permission first. Dreams cannot be worked on successfully unless there is trust between the dream-teller and the dream-listener. This alliance is a vital part of the process.

4. Time

Allow the child to express their feelings about the dream and its story by going at their own pace. Do not force the child to go on talking about the dream when they want to stop. Respect the child's right to draw the boundary and stop when they have had enough. Remember you are not a psychoanalyst but a supportive adult in a non-clinical setting. Most children need a grown-up friend, not a therapist.

5. Make links

Help the child to make links to events in waking life. If they have an upsetting dream gently try to help them discover what it relates to. Children can become much more aware of internal psychic pressure by working on dreams.

6. Dispel myths

Some children believe that if they talk about a dream then it will come true, others believe that if they fall in a dream, and reach the bottom of their fall, they will never wake up. Adults as well as children have asked me if these things are true. Help children to understand what dreams are and why we dream. They will then be much less afraid of their dreams.

7. Active dream work

If the child wants to, and it seems appropriate, encourage more active ways of working on dreams:

DRAW A DREAM

- Ask the child to draw the dream.
- Look at the picture together.
- Ask the child to talk about it, to explore it.
- Ask the child 'Would you like to change it?'
- 'If so, how?'

The child might want to have their dog with them, so let them draw in the dog. They might want to have a terrifying monster destroyed, so let them colour over it or cut it out. Be guided by what the child wants to do, do not impose your ideas. You can offer positive ideas drawn from the child, and help them to identify strong supportive figures, for example, who is their hero? Who makes them feel safe? Who or what could protect them? The aim is to generate positive responses to dealing with whatever has caused the distress. And where the waking event cannot be undone, use the dream action as a basis for discussion.

DREAM DRAMA

- Act out the dream.
- The child becomes director/producer/stage manager.

During the preparation of the drama, help the child to identify ways in which the dream could be more manageable. Encourage the child to identify support that could make the dream more bearable. If there is a dream character who is now dead or living away, perhaps they could talk to them or write them a letter that will not be posted but will express the feelings the child needs to communicate. The aim is to help the child face the pain or distress, and with your support find a positive way of dealing with it.

Dream sharing can be an ideal way of talking about major events in a child's life. It can be a very tiring, painful process so do not underestimate the affect such work may have. Given plenty of uninterrupted time and attention, this kind of dreamwork can drastically reduce the stress the dreamer faces in their waking and sleeping life.

CHAPTER 6

The Strain of Illness
'Dandelions Floating on the Wind'

Many children are fearful and shocked when they become ill. As well as feeling sick and having to take foul-tasting medicine, children see strange things happening to their bodies, the blisters of chicken-pox for instance or the rash of measles. They look to adults to explain and assure them that they will be well again. I remember my six-year-old daughter bursting into tears as the chicken-pox popped up all over her body. She stared at them in a mixture of amazement and horror, saying, 'I don't like them. Will they stay forever? Please make them go away!' It was relatively easy to reassure her, to tell her that most of us get sick as we grow up, and that she would be better soon. There was a typical time span for the illness and an easy diagnosis and treatment. Unhappily, this is not always the case.

Illness is a natural part of growing up, children are at greater risk of disease since their immune systems are still developing, and their immaturity increases their susceptibility to accidental injury. Though the onset of illness may be sudden, we anticipate some illnesses, such as measles, and wherever possible children are protected by vaccination. However that is not always possible given the unpredictability of life. Later in this chapter we will look at the impact of life threatening illness on children and families, but first let us turn to children's reactions to hospitals, which can be problematic, as it was for Josh.

Mary was delighted when her husband gave her a kitten for Christmas; and her five-year-old son Josh was thrilled with it too. However the kitten became ill, and though it was given all possible treatment, Mary finally decided that the vet was right and that it had to be put down. Mary explained to her young children that the kitten would have an injection to put it to sleep. They took it quite well, and after a few months when Josh had to go in hospital to get his tonsils out, no-one was thinking about the kitten. As Josh was being prepared to go to theatre, lying on the trolley, the nurse told him he would have an injection. Mary explained that the injection would make him go to sleep so they could take out his tonsils. At this he panicked and began to cry saying, 'No, I don't want them to give me that. I don't want to go to sleep, I want to wake up again.'

Fortunately Mary was there to quickly work out what he was so anxious about and to clarify the situation, though it took some doing. Josh believed the injection would kill him and like the kitten he would die. His mother was there to explain and eventually he was calm enough to undergo his operation. When parents are involved in the care of their children in hospital, the children reap the benefits. Babies and young children sleep better, cry less and when awake and have more company than they would otherwise (Cleary 1986). This continuity of care from the parent adds security to the child's world and aids recovery.

Children, especially those who have not been adequately prepared, have fears about hospitalisation. No matter how minor the procedure may be, to the child it is taking place in a strange place, with strange smells, sounds, furniture, and most of all strangers, who might be wearing white coats. With very young children this may be particularly difficult but there is no reason why even they cannot go some way to becoming familiar with the hospital prior to treatment. Stress is reduced where children are given information about what is going on, as we know from the results of research into how children are prepared for hospital treatment (Cline 1974).

The best systems do not gloss over the facts, but admit the truth, for example that having a blood sample taken 'hurts a bit'. Hospital-oriented play and the use of dolls, stethoscopes, plasters, surgical masks, appropriately linked colouring books and so on, let the children see what happens. Videos are used in some pediatric units to allay fears by showing admission procedures, ward routines and simple treatments. The optimum time to show such information videos to children over seven years old is about a week before admission, and for younger children just a day or two before. Where the child portrayed is of approximately the same age, sex and ethnic group as the child watching, they can identify more closely and feel less isolated. They see someone just like themself going through what will happen to them – and surviving it.

This type of pre-admission session, as well as reducing the child's anxiety, gives parents reassurance too. Certainly where children have had videos and booklets prior to hospitalisation, there is an overall reduction in stress (Samson 1988). In Dudley Road Hospital, Birmingham, the pre-admission programme has proved to be so effective that they have introduced an added bonus – they now invite the brothers and sisters of the patient to attend so that even more children can learn about the real life of hospitals.

Parents are much more likely to discuss and help prepare a child for hospital when they know what is going to happen and, as has been shown time and time again, if parents are less anxious, so the child is less apprehensive. Anxiety inhibits recovery so it is important to do everything possible to reassure the child.

If parents can stay with their children, take part in routine care and generally be involved, then anxiety provoked by separation, especially terrifying for young children, is minimised. If a child is suffering from separation anxiety it will make their hospital stay much more distressing, but most hospitals now recognise that continued parental contact with the child is vitally important and follow the National Association for the Welfare of Children in Hospital (NAWCH) Charter (2). This states that children in hospital shall have the right to have their parents with them at all times provided this is in the best interest of the child, and parents should be enabled to do this by having accommodation available. The parents have a mine of information that can be used to assist the child through the stressful experience and back on road to recovery, so their continued involvement should be maximised.Enid remembers 'the old days' when things were quite different: 'In those days when you went to hospital they wouldn't let your Mum or Dad come to see you. I remember – I was about seven – being in a cot in a bathroom. I didn't know what was happening. It was strange, cold, clinical. No mother. No-one to talk to. No curtains or furniture, and no explanation.' She still recalls the fear 30 years after her stay in that white-tiled isolation ward. She believed she was sleeping in a bathroom deserted by everyone she cared for.

Good child care in hospitals now involves explanations, a lot of listening, and encouragement for children to express their feelings, as was the experience of Nicholas, who had appendicitis, shingles and then glandular fever, all of which took him to hospital. Now aged twelve he suggested that children going into hospital should take a special toy with them so that they could get to sleep easily. Recently he has been diagnosed as having ME (Myalgic Encephalomyelitis, also known as Post-Viral Fatigue Syndrome) and must rest. Nicholas is getting used to the fact that he has little energy and cannot play football which he loved. He did not tell his friends at school about the ME in case they teased him and spread it around – they said often enough that he was just pretending to be ill so he could stay off school. Sadly he felt that somehow it was shameful to have such an illness, so only his family, teacher and doctor know of the diagnosis.

Every year some 1500 children in Great Britain are diagnosed with cancer, and more than 60 per cent recover completely with early diagnosis and treatment. For leukemia, the most common childhood cancer, the recovery rate is 90 per cent. However it is still a major life crisis for the sick child and their family. It is a formidable threat that no parent ever wants to face. Naturally there is fear of the illness and painful procedures the child will have to undergo – it may involve months of aggressive radiotherapy and chemotherapy with grim side effects and relentless stress. It is a perilous journey for the family, let alone the child who has the disease.

This stress is compounded for sick teenagers. At that age, just as they are gaining independence, their burgeoning autonomy crashes to a halt whilst friends continue to develop lives separate from their parents. The adolescent cancer sufferer has to bear not only the disease itself, but because of the reduction of control in their lives they have to relinquish newly acquired independence. They may also experience a reduction in confidence as their physical appearance changes through loss of weight or baldness due to drug therapy.

Frederick told me about the effects of his illness: 'I had to miss all games and P.E. lessons and after-school activities. I felt I wasn't as good as the others because I couldn't do the activities the other children could.' He was saddened when his friends used to forget and ask him if he was coming to play football when he had no stamina to join in. That feeling of being unable to take part is largely gone now, but sometimes he has to go to hospital and once again that prevents him from doing things with his peers. Frederick's illness curtailed his freedom, for other children over-protective parents may intervene.

It is difficult for the parent of a child with a life-threatening illness not to be over-protective. There is often a compelling desire to protect and indulge the child which can lead to stifling over-protectiveness. The needs of other children in the family have to be considered too. Catriona, whose sister was the centre of attention in the family as she fought for her life, became less and less confident. She withdrew into a shell that kept her trapped in silent hurt and at times she wished she also had the disease so that her parents would remember that she was still part of the family. Illness inevitably touches all members of the family in ways that can be divisive, the feelings of isolation and rejection that the healthy child experiences often go unnoticed.

The reaction of other people is another factor to be taken into account. As one mother told me, 'Having a child with terminal illness is like being bereaved. You don't know how to tell people the awful news and then they don't know what to say or do. Instead of avoiding you it would be so much better if they just came and gave you a hug if they didn't know what to say. I knew when my son was diagnosed that no-one could make the pain go away but I just wanted to know they were still there. I didn't want to feel abandoned.'

The experience of isolation for a parent can be devastating and Jane, whose story follows, has little contact with friends or neighbours. Her support comes from the social worker at a nearby hospice and the community nurse. Her words are quoted at length because they have important implications, for anyone working with children, about the way we give information and the manner in which we relate to those who experience loss.

When I met Jane she was caring for her fifteen-year-old son in the living room of her house. The room looked like an intensive care unit with a hospital bed and assorted monitors taking up the majority of the limited space. The regular high-pitch bleeps from one high-tech machine recorded information which showed the liquid food being fed through the nasal tube was not causing any breathing difficulties for Richard, the patient. He could choke if the feeding went awry – that was just one of the countless things for Jane to worry about. She explained what had happened:

> Two years ago I came home from work one day and everything was normal, nothing different. I'm a children's nurse in a specialist ward and I'm used to illness, but something strange happened. Richard said he didn't feel well and was going to lie down. About fifteen minutes later I went up and found him on the bed, he'd obviously had a fit and was limp and floppy. He was difficult to rouse, really hard to bring him round. I couldn't work out what it was, so I decided to take him to the hospital. They couldn't say what it was and ran some tests. But I couldn't understand it. He had been a bit tired over the previous couple of months and not eating very well, but nothing more. Then they said he must have been glue-sniffing and was attention seeking! Look at that picture. That's him with the St. John's Ambulance group. He was the youngest member and that's him being presented with an award by the mayor.

The strong, smiling young man in the photograph bore little resemblance to the thin, gangly, uncontrolled body laced with tubes. There was so little to show that they were the same person. Unlike Jane I had not witnessed the transformation. 'I was furious. That wasn't my Richard they were talking about. He still wasn't well, not right. When I got him out of that fit he was really bothered by the light and I told them that, but nobody paid any attention.' After his mother had fought tooth and nail for further tests to be run, Richard's condition was finally diagnosed:

> I found out, not in a very sensitive way, but I found out. I was walking through the hospital where I work, coming through one of the doors, when I met the consultant, the specialist who had seen Richard and done a brain

scan. I was coming through one door and he was just coming through the other, and there, as he held the door open to go through, he said, 'Oh, by the way, we've had the results on Richard and it looks like it's degenerative. Changes in the brain. We're not sure what it is yet but it's obviously some genetic dysfunction. Let you know what's happening.' And that was it!

The disease, eucodystrophy, affected the 'wiring' of her son's nerves. As she stroked his hair in that small room she explained calmly: 'He's doubly incontinent. He can't walk. We think that his brain isn't functioning, though now and again I have my doubts. I sometimes think he knows more but maybe he feels it by my vibes. I don't think he can see and he can't do anything for himself, and I don't know how much longer he can go on. I don't think it can be much longer.' Waiting, expecting Richard to die at any point, Jane has little support from her husband. They don't talk about things any more. They are two people living in one house separated by emotional pain and physical illness. The enormous pressure on the whole family has been almost intolerable. Charles, their younger son, is eleven now.

When Richard was finally diagnosed she talked to the specialist:

It was one of those million-to-one chances they said, but then nine months later Charles – he's at school at the moment, he goes to a special school now – started with the same symptoms. He started having problems with his sight, and in fact went blind within a matter of weeks. They managed to keep him in his ordinary school until the end of that summer term, but then he's had to go to the special school. Then last week he started having trouble walking and I don't think he'll be long out of a wheel chair. I don't know what I'm going to do then. I can't have two beds in this room can I? There's no space. I don't know what will be best. I don't know whether Richard's going to live that much longer anyway.

Talking to Jane, watching her thoughtfully care for and talk to her son, matter of factly check his monitors, was deeply disturbing. No-one could be untouched by her unstinting devotion, yet I wondered how she coped. How had she managed to face the grief involved, not just in one illness and impending death, but in this situation where her younger son who has seen his brother become completely disabled, is now afflicted with the same incurable disease. She told me, 'When Charles began to be ill, before his brain was affected he turned to me one day and asked, 'Have I got the same thing as Richard? Am I going to die?' Jane said she did not know what to say and in some ways regrets her reply, which was 'Yes, I think you have got the same but I don't know what's going to happen, but we're going to be here and we'll look after you.' She continued, 'I did all the right things, gave all the right assurances, but Charles was mad, really angry, and gave us four weeks of hell. He screamed, he fought, he hit out and railed against this world that was so unfair to him and his brother.'

At the time it seemed like the nightmare would have no end. Then about the fourth week they were driving in the car with both boys in the back when Charles turned to Richard and said, 'How will we recognise each other when we're dead?' 'Of course,' said Jane, 'Richard couldn't answer but Charles carried on, "I know, we'll be like dandelions floating on the wind."' He had smiled and held his brother's hand as if sealing a contract.

That moment is precious to Jane. That moment of acceptance, recognition and belief in a future which they, the boys, would have together, sustains her. As she rearranged Richard's wasted legs to ease the pressure, while she waited for her other son to be brought home from school, she said, 'That's how Charles felt before he lost touch with our reality, it was just a few days before his brain was affected by the disease. Since then Charles has become a happy sort of child. He still goes to school but he doesn't really know what is happening around him, and doesn't seem to be aware, consciously anyway, that he will die.'

In a way that's why Jane said she regretted telling Charles that he had the same condition as Richard, because Charles would have reached this stage of his illness and never needed to know. But he could see for himself that he was developing the same symptoms, so to lie to him would have been a betrayal. As it was he went through his mourning and found a resolution, an acceptance. Had she not told him he would never have known the importance of dandelions floating on the wind.

Children notice changes, just as Charles did, and they try to make sense of them. For example, if a child is in hospital and their mother keeps crying, and their father keeps taking days off work to visit, and everyone is buying presents, and even their normally combative sister is nice to them all the time, then the child senses that something extraordinary is happening. If no-one explains what this is they will probably build up a fantasy picture which may be far worse than reality. The knowledge that the rest of the family are keeping secrets can distance them to a lonely exile which makes coping with their sickness much harder.

Lack of information increases the child's distress. If children have no reliable information to explain the change in their parents' behaviour it leads to increased feelings of exclusion. Some children feel that the illness is a kind of punishment, or they feel anger towards parents who have not protected them from it or the painful treatment they must endure. Others feel a bewildering sense of injustice that such a terrible mishap should have befallen them, as Charles did before he became too sick to say so.

Children with life threatening illness differ from each other just as much as a healthy group of children do. Most important of all though is that they are children. Children are naturally curious and they want to know about their illness, how it will affect them and what the treatment will be like. Clearly spelt out treatment plans, however short term, will help the child manage the effects of at times unpleasant, confusing and painful procedures. Many children find the side effects of treatment worse than the disease, which makes it particularly important that they are told the reasons for drug treatments and the anticipated side effects.

I'm Still Running, written by Tracy Wollington, is the title of a powerful personal record of her fight against lymphona (Wollington 1985). I have included many of her own words because they so clearly communicate her response to a life-threatening illness that other children may feel but cannot, dare not, communicate. She wrote her book when she was fourteen and initially it is her earliest knowledge of her illness about which she writes:

> The clearest and most definitely the worst memory is that of the chemotherapy treatment. It was extremely awful. At nine it was difficult to understand how people could say that something which made me feel so very ill would make me well again. Because at that time I did not understand the effects this treatment was having on my body, it seemed a stupid thing for people to say...
>
> I had my treatment every three weeks and for the three weeks in between each treatment, all I could think about was the treatment that lay ahead and that scared me. It was reassuring to know that in two years time all of this would have finished. I had a goal to aim for, something to work towards. And the most important fact was that it kept me going to reach an end and hopefully a reasonably normal life, or so I had been told. Every three weeks I had one less treatment to go.
>
> I knew little about my illness at nine and took it for granted, it was like something most people had been through sometime during their lives, rather like any other common illness. It was just treated in a different way. I also hated having to have all the intravenous injections, blood tests and the pain that went with them. Near the end of the treatment this was particularly bad as I knew that they would have to search for a vein and maybe even try three or four times before they eventually did find a vein that was suitable. I think that all of the previous added to the fact that I always vomited before I had even received any treatment. All I could think

about was that for the next few days I would be constantly vomiting, stuck in bed connected to a drip and feeling extremely ill.

Tracy lost her hair and was completely bald for two years, but unlike some children, it did not bother her too much. Her family and friends made no embarrassing comments and that helped her to cope. Many children mention hair loss as the most upsetting part of chemotherapy. It is an obvious sign to themselves and their peers that they are seriously ill. It makes them look different and children are desperate to fit in with their peer group. People stare in supermarkets, children back at school make unkind comments and general insensitivity causes unwitting distress. Some children may prefer to wear a wig but whatever the choice the child needs to feel they are still attractive and still loved.

As there is a reduction in the ability to ward off infection following many cancer treatments, it is advisable for the patient to stay away from places in which there are avoidable risks. This meant that Tracey stayed off school for a year and was taught by a home tutor. However staying in touch with her friends was one of the most important sustaining factors throughout her illness.

Tracy went into remission when her treatment finally finished and after some time she was told just how ill she had been. She understood all that was behind her, and yet like so many other cancer sufferers, deep down she was still afraid it might return. As remissions lengthen anxiety decreases somewhat, but everyone worries about future survival. Tracy went on to enjoy the normal life of a teenager and even took part in the school nine mile mini-marathon. However when she was fourteen she once again developed worrying symptoms:

> I feel I should tell you about something that has proved extremely helpful to me. I wanted to know everything that was going to happen to me or what was happening to me…I was older and did not want to be kept in the dark. I needed to know as much as my parents knew. I hated the doctors talking to my parents in a separate room and talking about me while I was not present… It was me and my body they were talking about and possibly my life in the future. I wanted to have a say in what happened to me. No-one could know or even try to think they knew how I felt or what I wanted for myself, only I could decide.

Children have rights too. They have the right to talk about their worries and seek information as it affects them, and adults have a duty to respect those rights.

Barbara Ward quotes research which shows that children dying from leukemia who knew that they were dying wanted to discuss it among themselves (Ward 1995). However, they realised that doing so would upset the adults around them, and so they did not do what they so badly needed to do. Carefully controlled studies bear out the facts that even young children with cancer are aware of the seriousness of their illness and the threat of death without being specifically told. It does not help such children if we adults effectively muzzle them. By protecting our own feelings we deny them the right to understand their own life. We who live on may have more time to learn, the terminally ill child's time is limited and so their need is more urgent.

There are more reasons for keeping children in touch with what others plan for them, ones which are much more pragmatic. Adjustment problems decrease when children are given the opportunity to talk about their disease (Macaskill and Monarch 1990). This in turn has beneficial effects on the child's response to their illness. Silence chokes us all. And children, like adults, need the opportunity to put their lives in order and to say their Goodbyes.

The ultimate pain of terminal illness within a family is potentially one of the most disturbing crises ever to be faced. Advance preparation may lessen the shock when death comes, since grieving will begin whilst the sick person is still alive, if indeed it has not already begun prior to the overt information being given. We know lots more than we are consciously aware of – our inner-knowingness ensures that. Shielding children from the dying, their own or another person's whom they love, denies them the chance to continue their relationship with the terminally ill person in any real sense. Whilst those in the know manage webs of well meaning intrigue to 'protect' the child from the truth, the child senses the undisclosed truth and frequently feels isolated and rejected. Sharing in the dying process can be a special time for both child and adult, as it was for Charles. It also means any unfinished business can be completed and resolved.

Tracy had cancer again but it took quite some time to find out that it was a very rare form of tumour. Her reaction on diagnosis, as she describes, was one of fear of the treatment and fear of the possible outcome. Her fear came out as anger and confusion.

Loss of confidence after her first illness, losing her hair and not being seen as 'normal' undermined Tracy's belief in her abilities. This is something which hits many children who survive serious illness. Perhaps we are too busy sighing with relief and celebrating recovery to notice just how much a child needs encouragement and support to regain former self-esteem. Tracy, in the midst of the anguish of her second cancer, felt trapped at times: 'I hated having to put on false enjoyment when I wanted to scream, shout and cry, yet the faces around me were smiles and happiness. It was so depressing.' Everyone was trying to put on a brave face when it looked as if time and hope for Tracy were running out.

Anxiety does initially increase as the sufferer becomes aware of the seriousness of their illness and continues to do so with the progression of the disease and with each hospital visit as it did at this point for Tracy (Spinetta 1974). An angry response is part of the grieving process as we saw earlier, and all those around Tracy accepted her anger and did not tell her to 'calm down' or control herself. Instead unconditional love and positive regard gave her the opportunity to work through the catharsis and reach a point of genuine acceptance. When new treatments brought no improvement, Tracy made a crucial decision: 'I decided that I did not want to die in hospital after months of being ill. I decided that I would like to have some time when I was well and could enjoy life with the people around me.' This was ultimately respected by her parents and consultants, and her journal on which her book is based is a moving testimony of her journey towards strength, self-awareness and acceptance of her life and death. There was spiritual growth and renewal as she came to terms with her illness and impending death:

> I have accepted death, after all everyone dies. I am no different in that respect. In a sense we are all born to die, the only difference is I realise this and want to do something with my space in between. I am ready, it is those who are not that I feel sympathy for. Everyone thinks they will be here tomorrow. Each day is precious and I know death will come. Perhaps that is something we all should realise. Death exists for everyone.

Tracy died shortly afterwards having used her journal and poetry as ways to express the conflict and final acceptance of her illness. She was supported throughout by a family willing to travel that achingly demanding journey with her. Her legacy can enrich us, can enable us to understand the stress children feel as they face the trauma of life-threatening illness, as well as the profound personal and spiritual growth that may also take place.

Journal writing, creative play, or artwork, all have a healing part to play by facilitating the expression of emotions. Journal writing is different from keeping a diary in that it is not meant to be a daily, historical account, but a record of the writer's thoughts, feelings and ideas. The journal keeper has the chance to keep these private or to share them with someone trusted who will listen and talk about the feelings, if that feels right. To have the privilege of sharing journal thoughts and feelings is a precious gift to be cherished.

Some hospitals have art therapists who work with children. If there are no trained staff available you can still encourage a child to draw and talk to her about the drawings. Children often express their fears very directly in their artwork and may use them to communicate with their family. Always regard carefully what a child shows you and recognise that they may be telling you in pictures what they cannot say in words. In a safe, non-judgemental atmosphere a child gains healing release through drawing. A basic caring attitude and a willingness to be open to the child's view will enable you to aid the child on their path through a distressing stage of their life. With young children or reticent adolescents, a helpful strategy is to talk about people or other content in the third person, for example, 'I see you've drawn a little dog, I wonder what he is feeling/thinking/planning to do next?' This gives the child some distance from the emotions yet still provides a chance for them to release feelings by projecting them onto the dog in their picture. This helps to alleviate some of the isolation and loneliness that sick children sometimes feel.

The majority of childhood cancer patients can now expect to reach long term remission and so the quality of survival is increasingly important. However there may be long term effects from the illness and treatment, which include physical impairment and psychological distress. Approximately seventeen per cent of long-term survivors will have some degree of handicap and children need to be empowered to deal with this positively. Whilst in the initial stages of diagnosis and treatment parents and children are supported by hospital services, however when therapy is over and the child is discharged this support often drops dramatically. Parents and children need ongoing support and counselling at appropriate points. Following treatment for cancer, anxiety, depression, problems of poor self-esteem, as well as poorer intellectual performance, are often found. This is hardly surprising given it is such a ruthless disease and involves such drastic, debilitating treatment. However if the family recognises this may happen they are forearmed and can support their child more effectively.

When cancer survivors are compared with others who have similarly experienced life-threatening illnesses, cancer sufferers have a much higher risk of developing emotional disorders, perhaps because of the illness itself or the nature of the treatment. Whatever the reason this is bound to increase stress felt by everyone in the immediate family. Communication channels need to be kept open within the family, for the sick child as well as their siblings. A supportive and openly communicating family are a great asset in combating cancer and its aftereffects. As well as treating the physical illness we have to ease the psychological strain.

One of the most challenging tasks for parents is to balance time and energy between the sick child, who may be in a critical condition, and the others in the family who have differing needs. There is no easy solution. Siblings may be very co-operative but at times they feel resentment and anger. What they want most of all is for their lives to be normal again, so whatever the parents can do to keep up routines and family life, the easier it will be for them to manage the strain.

Given that the family may be stretched almost to breaking point by worry and tiring hospital treks, support from the extended family, neighbours, school and the local community should be sought. If parents do not ask for help people usually assume they can manage and may not take the initiative to offer. Others who have been through a similar experience, travelled that fearful road, may be able to offer the light of their experience to illuminate the way forward. Encouraging individuals to use these groups and making such introductions is a very important aspect of working with those who have experienced loss. (Resources and support networks are listed in the final chapter.)

Much more effort is put into the psychosocial support of children with serious illnesses now. No member of the child's family is left untouched by the child's illness and no family is left unchanged. Life-threatening illnesses are a family affair and how the family copes will be reflected in how the child copes. If parents of children with cancer cannot come to terms with the illness their child may suffer more. Thus helping them find a place to get supportive counselling, somewhere to express their fears, so that they can manage their own stress successfully and come to terms with the implications of the child's illness, is vitally important. Depression may develop in the face of unremitting pressure and it is to that we now turn.

Depression

Clinical depression in childhood is a real illness and is much more widespread than many adults realise (Nuffield Child Psychiatric Unit 1995). The signs, which may include anxiety, withdrawal, sadness, loss of energy, insomnia, academic failure, distress in social relationships and loss of appetite, can be easily overlooked or misinterpreted. It is especially easy to miss this when combined with other types of behaviour such as hyperactivity or delinquency. Such feelings come and go in a child's life, but should be treated seriously and counselling provided if they persist. This referral to professional help is not a criticism of parental abilities, but a recognition that it is often easier to talk to someone outside the family when there are problems, particularly where conflict within the family is inducing the stress.

A prolonged sense of helplessness and unhappiness are alarm signals that should alert any caring adult to the danger of childhood depression. Depressed children talk of feeling unloved, feel they are failures, have all sorts of fears and phobias and obsessions. Whilst these may preoccupy the child, the parents may be completely unaware of the child's true feelings. However, in the above mentioned Newcastle study into childhood depression, parents did report exaggerated illness behaviour, hypochondria, and increased appetite. By drawing attention to poor physical health, the child is really crying out for help with emotional distress.

Depression, which arises when the child's stress-resistance systems are overwhelmed, is different from ordinary unhappiness because the child experiences themself as isolated, as being apart from others. In addition they may see themself as being not good enough, or bad/evil in some way. Depression is often handed down from generation to generation, children learn to respond by seeing how those closest to them react. This learned behaviour, learned hopelessness, is every bit as powerful as genetic influences. Consistently research shows us that if a child has parents with psychological disturbance they are more vulnerable to life stress. Significantly there is a high correlation of depression between mothers and their children.

Another important factor is the link between childhood depression and marital discord. Mia Kellmer Pringle (1980) of the National Children's Bureau, after studying the affects of divorce, said that divorce should be on demand if you did not have children, impossible if you did because of the problems she saw for the children involved. Sometimes children react to this kind of stress by developing psychosomatic illness. Many workers with children have residual doubts about the veracity of psychosomatic illness, believing it to be fake in some way. However, emphatically it is every bit as real as an organic illness such as pneumonia, and is as painful and debilitating as other illnesses.

Anna, a thirteen-year-old girl came to me for counselling because she could hardly walk, and no-one could discover an explanation as to why she was in such pain. Her mother explained that the previous week Anna tried to walk after she got out of bed but almost fell over. The doctor could not diagnose the cause so she was sent to hospital for observation and investigation but no organic reason for her condition could be found. Eventually she was sent home until referral to a psychiatric ward could be completed. In a bid to avoid her child being given psychotropic drugs her mother asked me to see her.

I saw both Anna and her sister who was two years younger and listened to them. They spoke at length about the break-up of their parents' marriage and about the pressure their mother was putting on them. 'She wants us to do better than everyone else just to show she can cope now she's on her own with us. She always tells us not to let her down.'

They saw quite clearly, as children often do, what the problems were and offered suggestions about how things could be improved. On the third session we all met and the girls, with their mother's agreement, explained how they felt about what had been happening in the last six months. Together they worked out a way of easing the pressure. Anna had no further problems with her leg and the hospital visit was cancelled. Once the pressure was lifted she could stand, literally, on her own two feet again, but that psychosomatic illness was as incapacitating as any physical injury would have been.

Children sometimes express or experience feelings that are being avoided by other members of the family, usually parents. This may result in psychosomatic disorders. Where no organic basis can be found then it is important to explore the dynamics within the family. Psychotherapy and family therapy may enable members to see how a child may take up a displaced burden of care.

Lack of communication between parents and children has also been associated with depression in children. As you would expect, children are distressed by those life events which put pressure on their parents: bereavement, job changes or job loss, moving house and conflict. As the number of stressful life events experienced by parents increase so does the incidence of behavioural problems and depression in children, even children of three and four years of age. The idea that children do not know what is going wrong is nonsense. A successful way of tackling the depression, and the lack of self esteem that goes hand in hand with it, is to ensure daily successful experiences in the child's life. In school, small, attainable goals will counter low self-concept, and both parents and teachers can systematically provide positive opportunities for the child to receive praise and encouragement.

The essential aim is to enable the child to recognise and value themself. If this means the adult has to lower their expectations to reduce the pressure on the child, then it is a small price to pay for their future mental well-being. The depressed child can be helped by family and friends who maintain as normal a relationship as possible and point out distorted thinking without being critical or disapproving, It helps to acknowledge that the child is suffering and in pain, without blaming them for their condition, or saying or doing anything that will exacerbate a poor self-image.

One effective strategy is the energising approach. When a child is showing signs of that low, 'droopy' stage, initiate a change of activity or help the child to complete a task already underway. School attendance should be encouraged as it helps to maintain a balance of normality, though of course it is important to ascertain how the child is managing at school. Some children are perfectly well adjusted in the school setting but are unwell in the family setting. Obviously, listening to a child is of paramount importance. When you can get to the cause of the depression, you have a chance to resolve the difficulties.

An illness which indicates that children have reached a point where they are not coping with their lives is childhood anorexia, far more common than most of us realise. Essentially it is a morbid fear of normal body size and shape. The main symptom of Anorexia nervosa is a relentless pursuit of thinness through self-starvation. It is not only food starvation, the anorexic tends to deny themself warmth, sleep or physical rest, and push themself to the limit, physically as well as mentally. Indulging in what is pleasurable becomes dangerous for them because it threatens loss of control and the anorexic desperately wants to feel in control.

Menstruation and growth may cease as an anorexic girl fails to eat. In some cases a starving daughter perceives that previously estranged parents unite in caring for her, the focus of attention is changed. Bulimia nervosa is characterised by binges of eating followed by self-induced vomiting or heavy use of laxatives. Both these illnesses have psychological causes rather than straightforward physical origins and anorexia nervosa is seen in a lot of children, boys as well as girls. As one young anorexic said, 'Food was the only thing I could control, it was the only part of my life I was in charge of.'

The earlier anorexia is diagnosed the better, but as ever we tend not to acknowledge what we do not want to see, and boys may fall through the net because anorexia is still seen as an adult female slimmer's disease by many who do not associate it with males or children.

The symptoms may be masked but steady loss of weight is the most obvious one. A common explanation given for their behaviour by anorexic children is fear of getting fat, even though objectively their weight is not excessive. However, most sufferers it seems, come from families where conflict is rife, where there are excessive arguments, or the extreme opposite, repressed hostility. In some families alliances between one parent and a child that excludes other family members causes difficulties, as does failure to communicate. Sometimes it is the presence of a parent who is excessively overprotective that causes problems, and for many of these children the root of their eating disorder lies in the dysfunctional relationships within the family which they seek to manage through food. At least by controlling how much food they eat they grasp one precious area of power, even though it might become a life-threatening destructive power. Food is a classic area of parent–child conflict, so it is not surprising that it should be the focus of this war of independence.

Whatever the nature of illness, be it physical or emotional, there is always some element of loss and fear. Children in particular are vulnerable to the emotional stress illness brings. To ensure their well-being we need to be aware of and responsive to their needs, so they may learn to cope with illness successfully whether their own or that of someone they love. There are strategies to ease the strain which are considered in the next chapter.

CHAPTER 7

The Traumatic Impact of Abuse, Suicide and Disaster

Where the chances of harming a child's normal development are concerned, it (i.e. incest or other forms of sexual abuse by parental figures) ranks higher than abandonment, neglect, physical maltreatment or any other form of abuse. It would be a total mistake to underrate the implication and frequency of its occurrence.

(Freud 1981)

Every tragedy sends out waves of shock. Those closest feel the impact first, then gradually the aftermath reaches those further and further away. Some tragedies are so shocking they affect the whole of a community, then the whole of the country, as happened in the abduction and murder of two-year-old James Bulger in Liverpool. His abductors were also children. How could this happen? In the horror of the heart-rending news, in the midst of the furore, one family had lost their young son through murder, and two other families had lost their sons in a very different way, a different kind of death. Abuse, death, trauma and post-trauma were all part of this tragedy and it is to these that we now turn.

Abuse in Childhood

Child abuse is, typically, physical, sexual and/or psychological, and is relentlessly democratic, occurring in all religious, racial and social groups. A child may experience all three forms but one is usually dominant in the abused child's life. The stress and trauma of sexual abuse causes grave damage and has long-lasting effects on children. It involves profound loss, as Bea related in her recollection of her childhood: 'My home was broken, my sisters were battered. There were constant rows and very little money. We had to stay upstairs out of the way. I do not think I knew I was unhappy.' Her whole childhood was one of fear and misery, survival was the issue, happiness was not even hoped for.

Clare, though outwardly managing her life well with a good job and caring husband, was inwardly a depressed, frightened woman scarred by her early childhood:

I suppose if I'm truthful I think most of my problems stem from childhood. I hate silence and I think it's because when I was a little girl, if I did something my father didn't like he wouldn't speak to me for days and days, and those days seemed like years. I can remember at each mealtime – breakfast and tea-time – my Dad was always a frightening figure, not so much at breakfast time because I felt relief that he went out earlier than us most mornings.

I always had school dinners and then dread tea at home. We'd all be sat round the table, I can never actually remember what I did wrong, but there was always a lot of shouting and we *never* answered back, if we did we got belted. I can remember sobbing and saying 'Sorry' and Dad would say 'Go away! You're no child of mine', 'Get out of my sight, I don't even want to look at you.' Then it would be 'Now you eat that food, and you'd better eat it all, or else! And then you get to bed and when you're really sorry I'll think about taking you back.'

I can remember continually saying sorry and being completely ignored, pushed away, and this would go on for days. I can remember vividly going up to him sobbing uncontrollably and saying 'Daddy I'm sorry. Please be friends and please talk to me.' And looking back it was only when you were completely broken that he would take you back.

I was always being belted because I wet the bed, and because I was frightened of being belted I wet the bed more. I can remember as if it were yesterday dreaming that I was on the toilet and then waking up terrified realising what I had done. I woke my sister up and told her, we shared a double bed and she said if you tell Mum now instead of waiting until the morning maybe she won't be so mad. So I did. I hated going into Mum and Dad's room. I was crying when I woke them because I was so petrified. I don't think she put the light on because everything seemed black, and I had to be back in my room before she came in. I was petrified in a corner and she was hitting me like mad on my head. I remember feeling winded and my head banging on the wall and her saying 'You dirty bitch! You filthy little bitch!'

There were many more incidents of daily abuse but one which stuck in her mind was the time her sister told Clare not to eat her tea, because it had been poisoned. Christine had overheard her parents having a vicious row during which her mother said she was going to poison them all. 'I was terrified to eat my food but was made to eat it by my Mum, and each day that went by, I remember thinking with relief that we were still alive. Such relentless pressure erodes a child's self-belief.

Emotional and physical abuse within the family was not the end of it for Clare, like many battered children her vulnerability was visible to other potential aggressors. She became a victim of sexual abuse when her friend's father assaulted her:

> The first time it happened I had gone to see my friend Dennis. I'd knocked on the door and was told to go in. There was only his Dad in the kitchen. Dennis was in the front room and all I can remember was being pulled really close and Dennis' Dad breathing heavy. He put his hand inside my knickers and no matter how I struggled he wouldn't let me go. He actually ran an old people's home.

Clare looked surprised at this, as if still finding it difficult to believe that someone in a caring profession could be an abuser. Unfortunately, a minority of people who work in residential homes, care establishments and allied institutions, including religious ones, do abuse children. Where children or colleagues complain about abusive behaviour of a member of staff allegations must be investigated thoroughly. Too many children's lives have been irreparably damaged because no one believed them or acted on their behalf.

Children are taught to trust others at the expense of believing the truth of their own experience, so instead of utterly rejecting the abuser or informing others who might give protection, children like Clare deny their own perceptions and believe that they are mistaken, or that they themselves are the guilty party, responsible for leading the perpetrator astray. Clare continued:

> There are lots of details I can't or don't want to remember. One incident I do remember that came to me in a dream, funny really but lots of details reveal themselves in dreams. I can remember being in the home. I'd gone to play with Dennis and I always made sure I was as far away as possible from his Dad. I heard his footsteps and ran and hid behind a big white linen bag on wheels. I tried not to breathe too hard in case he could hear.

The abuser was a friend of her parents and they encouraged Clare to spend lots of time over at his house or the residential home, in fact they insisted she went despite her reluctance. How complicit they were in this abuse is not known, but they were not available to protect Clare since they too abused her, albeit in a different way. Who could she turn to? Like so many abused children she felt there was no-one she could trust to listen to her and protect her. As an adult she is now tackling the legacy of abuse which has resulted in recurring bouts of crippling depression.

When I asked thirteen-year-old Gareth why he had never told about the sexual abuse he suffered he explained he was ashamed and confused. 'Somehow because an adult persuades or forces you to do something and tells you it is right not wrong, and because he is in authority, somehow it must have been right.' This cognitive distortion destabilises the thought processes of young people like Gareth. It is part of the weaponry of the abuser because it confuses the abused, blurs the boundaries between right and wrong, and enables the perpetrator to keep power. The general rule for many children is, 'If an adult tells you to do it, then you do it,' particularly when the person is known to you as most perpetrators of abuse are. 'Then,' Gareth went on, 'that authority figure says it was your fault anyway and you believe them and that you've got to keep it secret or you'll get the blame.' Research evidence supports this view, showing, as it does, that the offender nearly always stands in a relationship of dominance to the victim. The added tension of keeping the acts secret and the allied fear of being found out intensify the extreme stress suffered by an abused young person.

Whilst there are few foolproof absolute indicators of sexual abuse, there are a number of signs that should alert you. This list, adapted from NSPCC guidelines for parents issued in an awareness raising campaign in 1997, covers the most typical ones:

- Disclosure by a child that they are being abused.
- Aggressive behaviour and severe temper tantrums.
- Personality changes, such as the child becoming clinging and insecure.
- Regression to younger behaviour, depression and withdrawal.
- An air of detachment or 'don't care' attitude.
- Overly compliant behaviour, watchful attitude.
- Sexually explicit behaviour which is not appropriate to the child's age.
- Continual open masturbation, aggressive and inappropriate sex play.
- Drastic change in eating habits.
- Inability to concentrate.
- Lack of trust in adults, particularly those who are close.
- Nightmares, sleep disturbance and bedwetting.
- 'Tummy pains' with no apparent reason.
- Medical problems such as itching, pain in the genitals or venereal disease.

- Running away from home, suicide attempts, self-inflicted wounds.
- Relationship between adults and children which are secretive and exclude others.

The abused child frequently feels guilt, self-loathing and fear and you may notice self-reference to this before you notice any of the changes above.

The child will use language he or she understands when explaining sexual abuse. For instance a child may say the man 'sort of sneezed' when describing male orgasm or may say that he 'wet himself'. If you encourage the child to tell their story in their own words without imposing the use of more adult, technical terms it will enable the child to feel confident and understood. Sometimes children reveal abusive relationships in their drawings and play (Burgess, Hartman and Kelley 1990). Learning to understand a frightened child's communication about this most painful of subjects can be a hard, painstaking task, and may well cause emotional distress for the listener. If you have cause for concern, first listen to the child, reassure, protect and get or give specialised help.

Disclosure is a process not a single event, and it may take a child months or years to reveal the extent of the abuse they have suffered. Only if they feel safe and protected from further abuse or retribution will they be able to express their loss. Throughout this time it must be stressed that only clear, unequivocal condemnation of the abuse can help to resolve the trauma. As with all recovery, consistent support, protection and reassurance are required to facilitate the process. Condemning the abuse is the first step in the healing process. Post Traumatic Stress Disorder, which is considered later in this chapter, may be another consequence of childhood abuse.

The reaction of adults when informed by a child that they have been sexually abused is crucial to that child's future. Children need to know that when they do tell they will be believed and protected, and that the adult will have the strength to survive. This feeling of strength is important because at the time the child may feel intensely fragile and be looking to the adult to 'lend' some of their power until the crisis is over or until they regain their strength of self. At disclosure it is essential to stay calm, to listen, and to thank the child for telling you. The child needs to know that you are not angry and that you recognise the effort and courage it takes to disclose abuse.

The degree of harm caused by sexual abuse depends on a number of factors including the age of the child, the relationship to the perpetrator, the intensity of the abuse and its duration. What is known is that it affects personality development and it may trigger off mental illness, such as manic or psychotic depressions and schizophrenia, where there is already a genetic predisposition.

Very early abuse, at two and three years old, can severely disrupt the child's still forming personality, leading to fragmentation of the child's perception of self.

Where abuse occurs in teenage years the abuse may become part of the young person's sexuality. Though they maintain more of a sense of their own identity than younger children, it may be more difficult to form close intimate relationships with others. Abused children blame themselves and sex becomes associated with guilt. Any child who has been abused needs to be given every opportunity to receive the skilled support of a trained therapist over an extended period to enable them to work through their experiences, and to limit any possibilities of this kind of long term damage.

Incest

Premeditated planned incest which is calculated to avoid any chance of the perpetrator ever being caught is widespread (Gordon 1989). Unlike people who batter children, most incest perpetrators express warped feelings of entitlement and justification or put responsibility onto the child. One young woman finally revealed an incestuous relationship with her father that had begun when she was about seven and ended when she tried to run away from home at fifteen. She told me that her father used to say he did 'special' things to her because he loved her most in all the world. He said it was a father's duty to teach her about sex, to show her what to do. He guarded her jealously, meeting her after school, taking her shopping, and refusing to let her go out at night because 'no boys can be trusted.' He never expressed any remorse and whilst waiting trial, bailed to stay in a hostel, he used to turn up in his works van and follow her down the road, calling to her and blaming her for his plight.

Young people often do not have the ability to refuse when pressured by adults to become involved in sexual acts, and the ripple effect damages other members of the family too. Families may be determined to keep an incestuous revelation secret from the victim's uninvolved siblings. Yet studies show that a year after the incest accusation it is the uninvolved siblings who are the most distressed family members (Kroth 1978). Whilst they may not be the immediate victim, their loyalties are torn asunder. Any child in the family who is of the same gender as the perpetrator is likely to experience increased concerns about the nature of their sexuality. We must always remember that the siblings become victims too, whether or not they were actually sexually abused, though all too frequently they will have been.

Children Who Abuse Other Children

It is well to bear in mind when a child tries to tell you about sexual abuse that not all perpetrators are adults. There is growing evidence that many child sexual abusers are children or young people themselves (Fahrenback *et al.* 1986). A study undertaken by the then Polytechnic of North London found that just over a quarter of cases are committed by under-eighteen-year-olds. ChildLine have many calls from young abusers who were themselves abused dreadfully, or who are being abused still. This behaviour is different from the exploratory 'nurses and doctors' games that children play, which are a normal part of development. However when such games include coercion or violence, where there are significant age differences between the participants, or where one child is forced to do something they do not want to, then it is not a 'game'. There is a big difference between two children experimenting and enjoying what is happening and an abusive situation where one child is being hurt by punching, name calling or threats by one or more others, and being forced to participate.

The National Children's Home annual report of April, 1992, reporting the results of their research in this area found that a third of people who sexually abuse children are under eighteen years of age. Perhaps this should not surprise us since the 'repetition compulsion' drives us to repeat what we have experienced. Alice Miller, expert in child sexual abuse, says, 'There is not one person who hurts or abuses a child, who has not been hurt or abused themselves' (Miller 1991).

Suicide

Death as a result of suicide is one of the hardest trials anyone has to face. As well as the responses to death we have covered so far, there are intense feelings of failure. Maybe, friends and family say to themselves, we did not love him enough, maybe we should have listened more, done more – the list goes on and on. These thoughts can torture the bereaved. Guilt is intensified if we also think that those around us, our wider circle, secretly or openly blame us for not preventing the suicide.

Sudden death for whatever reason is often harder to take than one which has been anticipated for a long time. Having had no time to prepare for the shock, those who are bereaved are often overwhelmed and traumatised. For children this shock is brutal, as it was for Morag.

Morag's mother committed suicide when Morag was six years old. Her brother James, then thirteen, came home from school to find his mother slumped in a chair. His efforts to revive her were useless so he rushed to a neighbour's house for help. James was in a state of shock. Morag was confused by the hive of activity that met her when she came home from school only minutes later, but no-one told her what had happened. Her two-year-old brother, who had been put down for an afternoon nap, was bewildered when he woke up, crying for his mother and upset by the noisy strangers in his home. Finally her father who was contacted at work returned. Distracted and in shock himself, he eventually broke the news that their mother had died but refused to answer any of the children's questions. Struggling as he was with his own tornado of contradictory emotions, he could not ease the distress of his children. However, the pain was compounded by the next series of events.

Morag and her brothers were hurriedly sent off, separately, to members of their extended family. They had no idea how long they would be gone, or what would happen while they were away, but Morag told me she thought they were being punished. By the time the children were reunited in their home their mother had been buried, their father had arranged support to help look after his young family, and he was again working full time. All the routines were back in the old order, the crucial difference was that their mother was gone.

Now a woman with three children of her own, Morag still thinks about her mother's suicide. For years she gnawed at the thought that she might have inherited some trait which would lead her to take her own life at thirty-three, her mother's age when she died. Only by learning more about her mother's life from her aunts has Morag managed to a large extent to be freed from her fears. For Morag and her father though there is a chasm of silence which continues to keep them apart. To this day he has never been able to talk about his wife's death.

Where a child has been touched by the suicide of someone they love, then all the caring strategies we have discussed so far are needed. In particular, all efforts must be made to ensure that feelings of guilt and rejection are clearly addressed, because those who are left behind frequently blame themselves, as we saw earlier. We need to empathise whilst ensuring that the child understands that suicide is a personal choice, either because of mental illness, the effects of drugs or chemical imbalance, or because the person felt their life was not worth continuing; and that that choice is not the responsibility of anyone else, least of all the child. In some cases suicide is the ultimate aggressive act which leaves intense anger in its wake, if this is the case the child needs the opportunity to work it through in a safe, supportive, non-judgmental setting.

Suicide Attempts in Childhood

Disturbing as it may be we have also to face the fact that some young people attempt to take their own lives. In America suicide is the second leading cause of death in the fifteen to twenty-four age group. Having to relinquish ties of dependency to parents and form close bonds with others causes great stress and upheaval. For some young people, perhaps as a result of mental health problems in the family, poor economic conditions, disturbed family dynamics and feelings of powerlessness, the task of living appears too difficult. This may be particularly the case for females who outnumber males in a ratio of 3:1 in studies of attempted suicides (Parker 1988).

Suicide is a way to alter or end stress. It is certainly not uncommon for children to have thoughts of their own death following the death of someone they love. For some it offers the best way to escape their pain, for others a way of 'joining' the lost one. Rosemary's letter in an earlier chapter shows her desperate longing to be reunited with her brother, which might have resulted in a suicide attempt. But what else causes children to take such drastic action?

The odds are that most adolescents will come into contact with suicide or attempted suicide in their school, their neighbourhood, or within the extended family. Of girls aged fifteen to nineteen, one in a hundred will attempt suicide in any one year. Not all those who attempt suicide want to die, many want a release from the distress they find unbearable, an impulsive act to stop the pain there and then. A five-year-old American boy, dying after being run down by a truck, whispered, 'It wasn't an accident. I figured if I died, it wouldn't hurt as much as if I lived' (Tysoe 1986).

The more a young person feels 'invisible' in their distress then the higher the chance that they will commit the highly visible act of suicide or attempted suicide as a way of drawing attention to the depth of their pain. It might be seen as the last attempt to leave a mark on a family or society that they feel alienates them. This feeling of alienation reveals that there is no-one they can confide in. In the early part of this century Durkheim argued that suicide rates increase as family, religious and political integration decrease. There are lower suicide rates among young people where there is a cohesive family unit and higher rates where families are experiencing disunity. (Hughes 1995)

Suicide can be an escape from an intolerable living situation or from a perceived loss. It is easy to think that teenagers are coping, that they are sufficiently mature, that they do not want any interference from parents, yet many find the fragile years of adolescence turbulent and distressing and do need parents to spend time with them, to talk, to listen, to be there. In many families communication becomes so strained that children take drastic action to get their plight noticed, their 'cry for help' is a lonely act.

The difficulty about depression in adolescents is that it is much harder to spot than in adults because of the mood swings that are common in young people during their adolescent transitional stage. If depression is prolonged or 'out of the blue' it should ring alarm bells. Warning signs put out by potential suicide victims may include some of the following: They may be withdrawn and unable to relate to others, have clear ideas about ways to commit suicide (perhaps linked to talk of 'sorting out' things/his affairs), talk of feeling isolated and alone, express feelings of failure, hopelessness, uselessness, dwell on problems that he can see no solution for. They may have in the recent past had a break up in a relationship, be facing unhappy changes in life such as illness, be involved in heavy use of drugs including alcohol, or be fearful about future changes such as going to college. Where there is a family history of suicide then the child might interpret this as the way his family resolves their problems.

Many suicide attempts are impulsive acts, so drugs within the home should be locked away. In a study by Dr Michael Kerfoot (1988), senior lecturer in psychiatric social work at Manchester University, eighty-six per cent of children between the ages of seven and fifteen admitted to Booth Hall Hospital for self-poisoning had taken drugs found in their home. Only one child out of a hundred had bought the tablets. Easy access to drugs can be life-threatening.

Self-injury is an important indicator in determining adolescents at risk of attempting suicide (Conrad 1991). If you are particularly worried about a child ask them if they have tried to hurt themself in the past. Approximately one in three girls and one in four boys reporting self-hurt behaviours may attempt suicide. In studies of children who have injured themselves deliberately when asked what would help prevent suicidal behaviour, the most common response was that a parent's show of affection and caring was the most important way to decrease suicidal behaviour. All too often adolescents who have chosen self-poisoning or self-injury as a way of expressing their distress have ceased to see the home as a supportive milieu.

Groups such as the Samaritans have a great proportion of telephone calls from those under twenty-five and ChildLine is inundated with calls from despairing children every day (Stubbs 1992). It is utterly devastating to lose a child through suicide for both parents and siblings. Support is available from the Shadow of Suicide Group (SOS), founded by Ken and Audrey Walsh whose fifteen-year-old daughter took her own life. It was totally unexpected for she appeared to have a bright future and was doing well at school. Somewhere along the line though her hidden feelings of isolation and poor self-esteem led her to her final act. After her body had been found on the railway track, her last note told her grieving family 'Tell everybody in the family I love them dearly and didn't do it to hurt them, honestly...I love you all and just didn't love myself, that's all.'

The stable, loving family, who spent time together, talked and enjoyed each other's company, where warm feelings were the norm, was devastated. There is still much work to be done on the chemical and hormonal changes that affect adolescents, and hopefully this will provide more knowledge about the causes of such suicides.

These acts are particularly traumatic because there is no warning, no ability to plan, and little empathy from others who are themselves uncomfortable about the suicide. Guilt, hostility, rage, anger, social stigma, emptiness and an extended period of self-questioning and self-recrimination must be dealt with. The stigma and taboo surrounding it often cuts off normal avenues of grief support. All survivors of a failed suicide attempt, from the child to his immediate family and teachers and other professionals involved, feel some responsibility. For the parent of a child suicide victim it is often the sign of ultimate failure and the worst condemnation of their ability to parent.

In Santa Mateo, California, there is help for children from the Suicide Prevention Centre. It not only offers telephone counselling but actively seeks out adolescents who might be at risk. The director and staff visit local schools, talk to teenagers about stresses they face and help them identify ways to cope. Young people have the opportunity to call about themselves or friends about whom they are worried. They can explore their concerns and find ways to deal with the situation. This interventionist approach is helping to keep down the number of adolescent suicides in the area and may provide a model for other cities to copy. In Great Britain the Samaritans are offering much in the way of support for young people and training for others who are concerned about them.

There is a strong link between severely stressful life events and suicide attempts. Life crises such as death in the family, separation, illness and so on, cause major emotional upheaval. Being too vulnerable under stress may lead to suicidal behaviour because it is a way of escape from unbearable pressure. On a simple level, if a young person is suffering increased stress there is an increased risk of self-destructive behaviour. And it is what the young person sees as stressful that is important here, not what adults see as stressful. For instance, whilst we may commiserate with a girl who had an argument with her boyfriend, we fail to accept that to her it may feel like it is the end of the world. Thirteen-year-old Orla expressed this intensity when she spoke of her dream: 'I found myself in a bedroom about to take an overdose of tablets because the boy I fancied hated me. My friend went to his home and told him about it and he came over and calmed me down. Then he asked me out and I was over the moon.' In working with young people we must take care not to trivialise these emotions otherwise we risk alienating those who need our support.

Every year in Britain over 100,000 young people below the age of seventeen run away from home or care. Voting with their feet, they run from serious problems of abuse, bullying, rows with parents, or from the wreckage of unhappy families. Or they may desire to seek a different life: whatever the reason they run because they believe things cannot be worse and with the hope that they might be better. Again and again such young people, once trust has been established, explain that they felt they were not regarded, not respected or believed, not talked to and above all they did not feel listened to.

The Children's Society provides a refuge in London for young people, and their work to date shows without a shadow of a doubt that these children are not running away on a whim or for trivial reasons but because the severity of the stress threatened to overwhelm them. Imagine you were a child whose parents had divorced, then the parent you lived with got a new partner who did not like you. Imagine that not only did they not like you but made life so difficult that you were eventually put into care, and then you had a series of 15 foster homes, each one being presented as 'your new home with your new Mum and Dad', and then you were abused by the foster parents: would you stay? This is not fiction, this is one young person's reality. Trauma such as this often leads to entrenched difficulties, which are considered next.

Post Traumatic Stress Disorder

Each disaster is different from the one before and the one after, the impact varies but we now know enough to predict the probable impact on those involved. After experiencing a major traumatic event, apart from obvious physical injuries victims undergo a variety of reactions.

Immediate distress includes physical symptoms such as nausea, fuzziness of the mind, palpitations, shaking, stomach upsets, diarrhoea and breathing difficulties, which may include choking feelings in the throat and chest. Head and neck aches, backaches and menstrual problems may arise. Feelings of sadness, shock, anger, helplessness, shame and profound fear are customary as are intense fear, helplessness, depression, lethargy and a sense of failure. Dreams and nightmares are characteristic of Post Traumatic Stress Reaction. Immediate psychological help for survivors following a disaster can significantly reduce the long term distress they suffer. The sooner de-briefing is offered the better. Such responses, it must be emphasised, are normal reactions to an abnormal experience.

These symptoms have now been recognised, medically and legally, as Post Traumatic Stress Syndrome (PTSS) or Post Traumatic Stress Disorder (PTSD) In addition there may be problems with concentration and memory loss. As well as phobia related to the traumatic event, relationships may be jeopardised as the individual withdraws into a cocoon, detached and estranged, or becomes subject to mood swings that alienate and hurt others because of violent emotional or physical outbursts.

Intrusive pictures, 'flashbacks' of their past trauma, may plague the affected child day and night, both waking and sleeping. In some cases the dreams are remembered whilst the original disaster is forgotten, but they persist and may cause a trauma in themselves. The disturbing dream or nightmare may be so realistic that the child wakes disoriented and in a cold sweat, believing that the situation is actually being repeated.

Directly after a traumatic event, apart from giving physical treatment for any injuries of course, the child needs reassurance that their feelings are normal in the circumstances and that they will eventually pass. It may be helpful to describe the automatic adrenaline response 'fight or flight' syndrome, which occurs when a person is caught in a crisis. Anyone involved in helping a child through this must remember that these reactions are not just 'in the mind' but are physical waves of emotion with a powerful force that can make the child dizzy or believe they are out of control.

Following disasters in Britain – the Kings Cross fire, the Bradford Stadium fire, the Zeebrugge ferry sinking, the Lockerbie air crash – the Critical Incident Stress Debriefing format has been developed. This is usually offered on day two or three following a disaster, day one is too early, and by day four defences may already be built up to deny the impact of the trauma. However, the family can be advised to listen to the child and be a supportive buffer protecting them from outside demands wherever possible, particularly if this involves intrusive media presence.

In Buffalo Creek, America, a slag heap engulfed a town leaving 125 people dead, hundreds injured and thousands homeless. Unlike a similar tragedy in Aberfan over 25 years ago, a systematic follow-up study was carried out with the children who were involved. They exhibited classic PTSD. Nightmares and sleep disorders were still prevalent among survivors two years after the disaster, nearly every child said that they were extremely frightened when they heard the rain or high winds because they thought the flood would begin all over again. Anxiety, belligerence and depression were widespread or intensified after the flood, and some children became preoccupied with thoughts of death and dying.

Similar reactions were experienced in children after a freak tidal surge smashed through the sea defences flooding Towyn, North Wales. Though for some the initial reaction was one of 'psychic numbing', six months later many children were still severely traumatised, weepy and with low levels of concentration.

The floods caused sewage to flow back from cesspits and sewers and long afterwards, some children were afraid of falling on the ground in case they became contaminated. Others will not sleep anywhere but in a top bunk bed whilst some small children re-enact the disaster by drowning dolls. Research into post-trauma stress in children found that children did not want to upset adults by expressing their feelings and encouraged the idea that all was well; but however well such feelings are masked children who have been exposed to trauma may need therapeutic support over an extended period, since their distress is anything but temporary.

Richard, aged thirteen, still has a recurring dream which he links to a traumatic event that took place when he was four. He explained what happened:

> It was the first of July and we were going to watch the bands. My Mum was washing my wee brother and my father took me out, up the street. There was a man sitting on a wall and he took me up next to him so I would be able to see. The wall didn't have any concrete, it was only built with sand and bricks and suddenly it collapsed. I was unconscious, I didn't really remember anything of it. I just remember a towel being put round my head, soaking up blood and the ambulance coming up the street. Then after that I was put in hospital, in intensive care, and I was near dead that night. My Mum and Dad stayed there all the time with me. I lost the sight in my left eye and went deaf and had nightmares every night. But it was all cured because my Mum took me to church and I got prayed for and all my cares went away after that.

The belief in the power of prayer and excellent medical care saved the child who had grown into this friendly, capable young man who told me his story. No visible scars or infirmities remain, only the dreams recur in which the wall repeatedly collapses but never injures him. The screaming and shouting are there in the background and the noise of the ambulance, but he is safe. He used to wake up shaking and screaming, feeling 'an awful baby for crying', but gradually, over the years, it has become much less distressing. His advice to parents whose children have dreams which make them cry is to tell them it's all right, listen to them, sit with them, and think how they would feel if they were having those dreams. Such inner wisdom is apparent in many children who have faced near-death experiences, and if we listen and respect them we can learn a great deal.

A delayed consequence of surviving a disaster is the feeling of 'death-guilt'. Those who live on fantasise that they have survived at the expense of another person or believe that they were meant to die and they will be threatened again until they too are dead. Such feelings have been described by survivors of concentration camps and Hiroshima as well by those who live through natural disasters. These long lasting responses indicate the need for continued support for children who have been exposed to such traumatic incidents.

The legacy of the attack on Hiroshima and Nagasaki, which killed tens of thousands of people who died at once, speaks on in the generation who survived scenes such as this one recalled by Futaba Kitayama:

> By my side, many junior high school students were squirming in agony. They were crying insanely: 'Mother! Mother!' They were so severely burned and bloodstained that one could scarcely bear to look at them. I could do nothing for them but watch them die, one by one, seeking their mothers in vain. (Lifton 1967)

Children who have been bereaved as a result of a sudden disaster such as a bombing or random attack of some kind, often have as high levels of stress as those who actually witnessed and survived the disaster. Diverse factors such as the tolerance level of the individual, the extent of their injuries, and the nature of their involvement, all play a part in the severity of the post trauma reaction. However bear in mind that a road traffic accident or a mugging can produce the same stress symptoms as warfare or a disaster. In working with children who have had traumatic experience we need to reassure them that their responses are normal and not a sign of weakness, nor a sign that they are going mad. Usually, those involved seek a meaning, a reason for the event, to try to make sense of it.

As with all PTSD victims, the key to release is in helping the child express themself and recount what they have been through. They need a secure routine and structure to their lives in the aftermath of trauma, to cope with the often terrifying effects already described.

Some children enure themselves to the distress of disaster by repeated mental re-enactment of the event, by repeating it in play for instance. In some cases the child imagines taking on a more powerful role, for example a child who was abandoned will throw away a favoured toy again and again, taking action rather than being acted upon, as they were in the actual situation that gave rise to their pain. Dramatic tragedy is based on the premiss that there is catharsis in playing out in disguised form the fears and misfortunes that beset humanity.

Terrorism and War

Whilst natural disasters are terrifying enough, human-made violence may be even more incomprehensible. Terrorist violence appears to cause longer-lasting and more painful mental consequences for survivors and relatives because they seem more senseless than natural events. How can you explain it to an adult, let alone a child?

The horror of war is inflicted on children all round the world, every day of the year. In the siege of Sarajevo, 1993, there were an estimated 62,000 children under the age of fourteen who were trapped, 1250 were killed and 14,000 injured; the number of those psychologically wounded is not recorded. These figures reflect only one situation – if you consider the conflicts before and after, as well as those currently taking place, then you see the incalculable damage being imposed on the children of our world which in turn effects the next generation.

Children who live with war may become so brutalised that they go on to perpetuate the vicious cycle of hatred and repeat the battles in adulthood that they experienced in childhood. Northern Ireland demonstrates that painful truth. Children in war, like many in Sarajevo, become aggressive, scream all the time, cease to speak coherently any more, and are terrorised by nightmares. In war neighbours become enemies, natural justice does not hold sway, no one can give complete protection, and so children's trust in adults is destroyed. They lose faith in the adult world. Their memories can be like a horror film that runs and re-runs offering no respite, a classic PTSD symptom.

When a person is abandoned and deprived of all support systems and there is the threat of death, – 'the extreme situation' as Bruno Bettleheim calls it – then support must come from somewhere if they are to survive. What has been found helpful is the maintenance of family bonds which unite despite the threat. This reassures children and helps them feel less vulnerable.

Teachers, counsellors, therapists and medical practitioners who work with children who have been exposed to war or the threat of war, need to allow them to talk about it, to talk about the news or the reality of the situation if they were caught up in military conflict. They need the opportunity to face their fears. Let them voice their feelings of confusion and powerlessness. We can acknowledge that war frightens us too, but show that we can live without being overwhelmed by that fear – we can show that we can continue with our lives. Life is complex and part of that complexity involves living with fear of all kinds, and living with ambiguity. Children who learn that it is acceptable to express fear will be far better able to deal with their feelings than those who are taught to repress them. This is developed more fully in Chapter 9.

The strain of being in a war zone and the need to escape is clear from Pamela's words. Aged thirteen and living in Northern Ireland in 1990 when I first spoke with her, she expressed the views of many of her generation who have never lived in peace:

As you must realise, the conflict in Ireland makes our lives different from other teenagers, not drastically but I believe our hopes and dreams for the future cannot be compared to those of children in England and Scotland. Most of us hold no hope for the civil war's end, so we will leave Ireland.

And with that, although there will be feelings of freedom from warfare, the negative side is that there will be a continuance of the theme with loss: loss of homeland, loss of close knit family support, and loss of their community and culture. Perhaps one of the reasons for the very high standard of educational achievement in Northern Ireland is because young people see good results in examinations as a way of escape to work or university outside Ireland.

This exodus from conflict has resulted in the diaspora of many ethnic groups, including Jewish and African as well as Irish. The diverse communities in the New World are living evidence of the power of conflict to de-stabilise and disperse whole communities from their homes. This historical fact bears importance for anyone who works with children, since they frequently carry the emotional scars of their parents' wounds. In some way they inherit the holocaust and we need to look out for and address this legacy when we see children or grandchildren of immigrants.

Loss in childhood may be unavoidable in many instances, but whatever the causes and whatever the nature of their loss, our children need to be able to rely on us to care enough to help. If we do not then the future will not be a good one for any of us. The continuing very high incidence of depression, loneliness, suicide and violent behaviour which are linked to inadequate care of our children will haunt us into the next millennia. We have a choice.

CHAPTER 8

Disability

During my research for *Helping Children To Manage Loss* I asked people to contact me if they had experience of loss in childhood and one of the most moving letters I received was from Tony. His letters expose the deeply painful choices that some families have to make. In Tony's case those heartachingly difficult decisions have had repercussions over many years and for all the family. His story is a salutory one, and he began with the 'bald facts':

> Emily is blind with Retrolental fibroplasia. She has a twin sister Megan with normal vision. They were both 12 weeks premature. She has an elder brother David who is twelve, Emily is ten. We live in a village five miles from a large city. David and Megan both attend village schools but Emily is forced to go to M. in the city, She goes out of the house three-quarters of an hour earlier than the other two.

The 'facts' set the scene and the juxtapositioning of Emily's impairment with her twin sister's good health intensifies the loss involved. Her father recalled Emily's first operation when she was five:

> We were a week with her in hospital in Cambridge. I remember having to physically hold her down in a waiting room full of people so the nurse could apply eye drops, and having to stand her screams because by this time she knew they were going to sting and hurt like crazy. And we have lost track of the times she has walked and run into things, the edge of the door especially, and all you can do is drop what you are doing and run to her, pick her up and hold her close and comfort her.

That early stress of physical pain is one that has recurred for Emily, but directly and indirectly her trauma affected all the family. Constantly on the alert to prevent such collisions, they lived in a heightened state of stress.

The emotional reality of schooling was and remained extremely distressing:

When she first started attending M. School it broke our hearts to see her go in a smoke filled taxi in the morning with uncaring people to an inner city school where we would never have sent the other two. The taxi driver was always late, coming to a skidding stop and bundling our Emily in because he had other pick-ups to make. It was stressful for us all and we finally got the taxi company changed, but it took months and months and it was the threat of withdrawing her from school that made a difference. Looking back on it now I don't know why we put up with it so long, but in our defence I ask 'Have you ever tried to get hold of anyone at County Hall? They are always in meetings and you never get past their secretaries.

Tony and his wife pushed for Emily to attend the local village school with her brother and sister. It was a long process involving the stress of statementing to assess her needs. At last they won the day, but although Emily was much happier it was, Tony felt, too little too late. By the time it was resolved Megan had made her own friends at school and wanted to play with them on her own without having to feel responsible for her sister every playtime. These conflicting desires 'tear her apart'. She feels guilty if she leaves Emily and resentful if she has to look after her and abandon her friends. Choices involve loss as we said earlier, and though Emily finished her early education at her local school she had then to face the prospect of middle school.

Now, at M. middle school, Emily gets home an hour later than her brother and sister, who by that time are already out with friends. Her life is totally different as Tony describes:

Emily goes to her bedroom, switches on the tape cassette player and strokes the cat and asks when Megan will be home. She is not integrated at home or at school and the education authority cannot meet her intellectual or musical needs – she is a gifted violinist. We want her to go to a new college for the blind in Worcester where her needs can be met, where she will be able to make friends on an equal basis and not told who to play with, as has happened in the past. We want her to go somewhere she can compete with her peers in sport and every lesson, and not feel different because she is the oddball. And where she can be taught the braille code for music and try for university, which is what she wants to do.

Tony's experience of integration into mainstream education leaves him upset and bitter:

Going back to Emily's social life, she made one friend at M. school in four and a half years, and that was Tim, another blind kid. Good integration isn't it? Unfortunately for Emily, Tim was allowed to go to Worcester at half-term last year, so she is isolated yet again. You asked about stress and loss: well all I can say is you should have seen Emily last term and at Christmas, waiting with dread the start of the new term, I don't think that kid's got any more tears left in her.

Whilst this was happening, Tony and his wife were preparing for their appeal to allow Emily to go to the special school to which her good friend Tim had transferred. However this had repercussions within the home, resentment was building up with their two other children because their parents were spending so much time with Emily. The atmosphere became so strained that they had a family meetings to try to sort things out. Both elder children burst into tears and said it felt awful because everything was revolving around Emily and no-one had any time to think about what was happening to them, and they cried harder because they felt guilty for feeling that way. No-one prepared the family for the stress that has dogged Emily's educational and social path. No professionals were available to counsel the family at the times when they were truly desperate as they were in this situation, or the time they came back from holiday.

It was 1990 and in July, camping in Germany, they were making plans to go to Berlin to get a chunk of the historic wall which had finally come down. They never got there because the night before, excruciating pain started in Emily's right eye, and they sat up through a tortured night until it subsided. Neither aspirin, codeine nor any other pain killer made a difference. Nights of abject misery and anguish continued after they arrived home until at last they had an appointment with Emily's eye specialist. The weekly visits culminated in three operations for Emily, the final one of which almost resulted in the loss of her eye.

The effect of all this was dramatic, Tony and his wife felt they aged immeasurably, Emily went from being a bright, bubbly girl to being a quiet, introverted person, missing lots of schooling on the way, and both the other children and the grandparents were put under enormous strain. The trauma of living with disability should never be minimised no matter how many people you work with.

No-one can be prepared for a tragic event that happens as totally unexpectedly as it did for Tony's family. But once the unimaginable happens then every possible support system should be available to ease the strain for all the family. Many cities do have more sensitive caring approaches when helping children and their families than that which Tony experienced, but anyone working in this area must inform parents of all the resources that are available, including voluntary organisations. Parents should be encouraged to communicate any dissatisfaction. Complaint procedures need to be in place and harnessed, as an opportunity to learn from any misunderstandings and mistakes, to improve services to families facing loss of whatever kind.

After the Birth of a Disabled Child

Where a child suffers acute or chronic illness, accidental injury, or where a baby is born with a disability, the loss impacts on the whole family, as Carole can confirm:

> Two years ago our fifth child Dominic was born with many problems, and he managed to fight, quite literally, for his life on more than one occasion. Dominic was much wanted after a gap of seven years and the pregnancy and birth were very difficult, and as we are a very close family we all leaned on each other, and everything was understood by and shared with the other kids. This is well highlighted: They all arrived at the hospital, fifteen miles from home, at 8.30am on the day I was to be induced. Wild horses couldn't have stopped them and my husband Alex was there of course. Dominic was born at 7.40pm and they were rewarded for their vigil by being able to meet him when he was only eleven minutes old. This was rapturous for them. So you can imagine the impact on them of what followed. I was completely unprepared for what happened myself, let alone know how to help them at this traumatic time. But it was horrific. We came through it eventually I think. We were just starting to get back to some kind of normality when at five months Dominic was diagnosed as being completely blind, with some areas of brain damage. Their reaction to this has been very, very hard to cope with or understand, and even now eighteen months later, things still aren't right. What I wanted to say to you is that there doesn't seem to have been any help for them – we are well supported with Dominic in every way – but I have struggled with the others and their hurt has just added to all the other difficulties. I really couldn't begin to describe everything but I really would have been helped by any information about the affect on siblings of this kind of thing, I would like to think I have helped my kids with lots of patience, time, and most of all love.

The birth of a child with a physical or mental disability is a severe shock for a family like Carole's who grieve the loss of the 'perfect' child they hoped for. Reactions may be ones of recrimination, guilt, anger or total rejection. All have a part to play in coming to terms with this loss, and just as with a physical death, you need time to mourn and adjust, as Carole describes.

How the news is given to siblings, and how it is accepted, can affect the entire future of the family and its ability to cope with the stresses involved.

Research into how and when to break the news of disability consistently shows that the earlier and more honest the approach the better, and plenty of time should be given for questions and discussion. The immediate response to learning about disability is traumatic for all concerned, and then there is the future. The family need to consider the plans and hopes of all the members, and develop strategies to help them move towards their goals, bearing in mind the changed demands.

The quality of life for a disabled child can be significantly enhanced where the right education is provided. This may take some fighting for, as Tony's accounts testify, but there are resources available for both the child and the family who do need support and respite.

Many national societies listed in Chapter 12 provide a range of services for children, their parents and those who work with them. These include advice, information and support, in-service training for teachers, social workers and other health professionals, specially adapted equipment, toys, books and tapes for children too. They can provide advice right up to the time of career choice and further education. Seeking support is one of the first strategies in regaining control when a family feel knocked off course. They learn that others have faced similar crises and survived. In many cases, not only survived but become strengthened in ways they could never have imagined.

The isolation felt by families when one of their children is diagnosed as being different, in need of special education for instance, is often overlooked. Yet one child in five is likely to experience learning difficulties in school. These include children with specific difficulties such as physical or sensory impairments and those with learning or behavioural problems. These may be catered for in special schools or within special units in mainstream schools.

The 1988 Education Reform Act stressed the need for a broad, balanced education for all children, and under the 1981 Education Act children with special needs should have a 'statement of need' which specifies those needs and identifies the resources necessary to meet them. 'Statementing', where a child is assessed and strategy determined as to how best to meet these needs, should ensure that the child is not overlooked. The statement is reviewed once a year and adapted to meet the developmental needs of the child. In some local authorities, peripetetic support teachers can be assigned to children in school to offer specialised assistance. Parents are crucial partners with teachers in the education of their children and their voice needs to be heard.

Susan, who was eight when I met her, has tunnel vision, a severely restricting visual impairment. When her sight began to deteriorate Susan told me: 'I dreamt about pulling my eye out. Mum put it in the bin and rubbish got on it and then I went blind. She took it out then and gave it to me, I put it back in.' But Susan did not regain her former sight and she had to revert to a much more dependent relationship with her mother, not an easy task for either. The dependency that children who are disabled feel and fear is easily overlooked. Many visually impaired children I have spoken to have dreams in which they are abandoned or in which parents are careless of their needs, so like Susan's mother they are held responsible in some degree for their child's disability. Parents are viewed as powerful beings so there are bound to be ambivalent feelings on the child's part about parental inability to protect them.

MOVE (Mobility Opportunities Via Education), is a programme for children and adults who have restricted movement because of severe and multiple disabilities. Children with cerebral palsy for example, are further disadvantaged because of of restricted communication, motivation, low self-esteem and lack of choice about what happens in their lives. MOVE, which has been used successfully in America for some time, emphasises the importance of mobility to enable learners to perform such activities as self-feeding and self-controlled toileting, as well as moving from place to place. There is a cumulative effect when children who arc confined to a wheelchair learn to stand, even for brief periods. People relate to them differently, it increases their self-confidence, parents experience new optimism and are encouraged to respect their child anew.

The scope of their progamme is beyond the remit of this book, but I include it because it focuses on the need for independence that all children have, no matter how limited their physical functioning may be. Whatever the level of skills of a child, as professionals we have a duty to address their emotional needs, even though physical needs may seem the obviously dominant factor.[1]

One essential act whether the illness is physical or emotional is to listen to what the child is telling you. Brent recalled:

From early childhood I had difficulty breathing through my nose. When I complained about this I was told to blow my nose or that I wasn't blowing properly even though I kept saying I couldn't. They said I'd grow out of it, that I was complaining about nothing, so eventually I gave up. Much later I was taken to a different doctor and he discovered that the bones in my nose were slightly displaced, so causing a difficulty in breathing through one nostril. I just wished someone would have done something about it sooner.

1   For more details contact Jenny French at MOVE International Europe, Centre for Educational Development, University of Wolverhampton, Gorway Road, Walsall WS1 3BD.

As it was Brent had to put up with the discomfort and embarrassment until he was a teenager. It certainly did not help his confidence. As a result he is always hesitant in expressing his own views because 'people don't listen.'

Children with special educational needs may be more at risk of abuse yet less able to communicate the fact. Disclosures are especially difficult because the only people in whom they can confide may be too close to the abuser, and many services will be inaccessible, though ChildLine has now opened a specially adapted line for deaf children, and the Royal National Institution for the Deaf have a number of advisers who can offer support on a whole range of issues.

Sex education may be inadequate, leaving the child in isolated ignorance. Some teachers, mirroring views held in the wider society, seem to believe that children with special needs or physical disabilities are asexual beings, and so do not need sex education: they do (Craft and Craft 1978). 'Kidscape' has had a campaign to address these problems and can supply information if you contact them, as can specialist groups listed in Chapter 12 (Mallon 1989).

Sexual abuse is rarely predominantly about sex, but rather more often about power, vulnerability and abuse of dependency, which means that the range of children at risk includes those with physical and mental handicap, however it is often more difficult for such children to communicate the nature of the abuse.

Family members when they learn of an assault typically react with feelings of rage and guilt and believe they should have done a better job of protecting the victim. A sense of helplessness and bewilderment arises as to how anyone could perpetrate abuse on a disabled child, combined with the fear of possible infection, pregnancy or emotional damage. The family need the same sensitive support and counselling that anyone else would when caught up in such tragic events, particularly bearing in mind that 'stranger-danger', that is abuse by a stranger, is less likely than abuse by a relative or care-giver. In one study, 99 per cent of assaults were carried out by the latter (Ryerson 1984).

The brothers and sisters of children who have a mental or physical handicap may find themselves more socially isolated at school and in their neighbourhood (Andersonn 1988). There can be many reasons for this, such as a strong emotional commitment to their parents and sibling which leads them to spend more time within the family, especially where their help is needed in caring for their sibling. The child may feel different and hurt by the prejudical intolerance that is still attached to disability. Children inevitably feel stress when there is illness in the family, whether it is physical or mental.

The stark statistics concerning children's mental health makes disturbing reading. A recent report by Dr Sophia Zeman, the Mental Health Foundation's scientific officer, stated that at any one time one in five children has a diagnosable mental illness; up to forty-nine per cent of children and young people meet the criteria for at least one mental disorder during childhood and teenage years, and there is evidence to show that more school age children are attempting suicide than ever before (Zeman 1997).

Mental illness in a family is sometimes concealed because of fear and prejudice, but this creates its own strain. The grandson of a schizophrenic grandmother recalled visiting her in a locked ward in one of those intimidating Victorian mental hospitals. Frightened, not knowing what to say or do when confronted with her illogical behaviour, he struggled to make sense of the situation. His parents made it clear that Grandmother was not to be discussed and the overriding message he got was that mental illness was shameful. Such attitudes are still prevalent though campaigns by mental health associations are improving awareness and breaking down barriers.

Martin's father was almost killed in a car accident. Then aged eleven and just starting at a new school, Martin found his world turned upside down. For weeks he, his mother and brother expected his fathers' death at any moment, but he survived and was admitted to a specialist hospital for spinal injuries. 'He will come home', the family were told, but six months later when he came home he was a very different man.

His head injuries caused brain damage which resulted in a personality change. Martin's father was now an unpredictable, violent stranger. His sons cowered in fear whenever his violent moods erupted. Although their local doctor knew of the predicament he could offer no respite because the father's abusive outbursts were random and not dangerous enough, he said, to warrant his committal to a mental hospital. The family lived in communal misery.

Only when the unfortunate man died ten years later did the family relax, but for Martin it was too late. He told me that his whole school life was blighted by his father's illness. The cumulative effect of missing so much early time in his new school, and then being constantly preoccupied with worry about the next outburst, left him feeling completely inadequate. He never brought friends home from school and felt isolated from them when they talked about their own fathers. He was ashamed to reveal the true situation, and avoided games in order to hide his bruises after beatings. That in turn caused problems with his PE teacher who had no idea about Martin's situation. But, he asked, how could he let his mother down by telling the real truth of his life?

Hopefully, today more support is available to children like Martin who are deeply affected by illness within the family. Increased sensitivity and awareness has led us to recognise just how deeply lives are disrupted when childhood is terminated all too abruptly. Living in a family with mental illness for instance, means that children have to take on burdensome responsibilities far too early.

Neighbours and extended family may not be there, so care in the community needs to take into account care for the children of patients as well as the patients themselves. Advice, respite and support are essential if children are to survive such experiences emotionally intact.

Not all accident injuries are as devastating as the one Martin's family experienced. Simon, now twelve, remembered the time his father broke his leg and was in hospital:

> I was five or six when it happened. I used to sit by the window at our old house, in the living room and watch out of the window and see if I could see him walking up the front path. If there was a thunderstorm I used to count between each thunder clap – that used to help me keep my mind off him. The worst part of it was my little brother who was only two just laughed at me when I cried.

Looking out for his father to come back home, waiting and watching, young Simon recalls no explanations. Some children do need more reassurance than others and need to visit hospitals to be sure that the loved person has not disappeared forever. The impact of unexpected separation hits children hard.

Children With Special Educational Needs.

Children who have poor cognitive functioning, either through low IQ or disability such as Down's syndrome are as affected by death as any other group of children. Whilst they may not be able cognitively to understand what has happened to cause loss, they still feel the profound changes it creates.

Steven, who was severely mentally handicapped and unable to communicate verbally, reacted strongly when his father left home following marital estrangement. His head-banging got worse, he began injuring himself and poking objects in his eye. All this in response to the pain he was feeling. Professional help was needed to cope with this extreme reaction. Thinking that the child will not notice is counterproductive. They still feel hurt and need the opportunity to work through their grief.

At one school I spoke individually to children with social, physical and emotional difficulties about their experiences of loss. Many of the pupils were in temporary family placements following a breakdown in parental care. There was wide experience of loss and in many cases the children drew pictures to help communicate what had happened to them. Clearly many were concerned about death and what happened at death. Far from immediately forgetting it, they were puzzled by it and wanted to know more.

Nine-year-old Peter, a child with mild developmental delay, lived in a family which was dysfunctional enough for him to be placed in foster accommodation intermittently. I have included his comments in detail because they reflect a number of concerns about loss for children who have special educational needs. He told me:

> I lost my hamster the other week and I was upset. It had these things on its back and it was sick. When I found it, it was dead...I felt very upset. I buried it myself near the rabbit. Them two were friends. I felt really upset and started to cry, because, you know, when I found it, it was in such a position. It looked like it had broken its leg or something... My Mum was there. She was a bit upset but she didn't cry.

It was important to him that even after death, the hamster should have the companionship of his friend the rabbit. Peter said that he felt a bit embarrassed about crying, but the burial was very important to him too.

He put the hamster in a plastic bag with its bedding and then buried it. He also put a rose, and 'the seed of a rose' on top of the filled-in grave. Rituals such as these, where a thing of beauty and the seed of new life are included, have been around since Egyptian times and earlier. They meet an innate need to both mark the event of death emotionally and physically, and to link death, the end, with new life, the seed, a beginning. The ritual of caring and marking the grave gave him the opportunity to do something constructive, to respond to death in a positive way. Talking of his pet led Peter to recall an earlier experience of death:

> My Grandad died...I'm glad he's safe but I didn't really want him to die, but he's safe in heaven now... My Gran and Grandad used to live in a house with stairs and they used to have to bring the bed downstairs. My Grandad was very old. He had epilepsy and was very weak on his legs...I think it's safer for him to be in heaven. That helps but he used to take me places and we used to have a bit of fun when I was smaller. He used to have some laughs with me.

I asked Peter if he went to the funeral:

> No, he was burnt and it's too upsetting but I heard about it, that he was in a white robe and they put bits of special make-up on him to make him look like he was alive. My Mum said I shouldn't go to the funeral but I really wanted to go.

As discussed earlier, children should be given the opportunity to attend funerals if that is their wish. Peter's common sense awareness of death and its impact, like so many other children I spoke to, could provide a good example for many adults to follow. When I asked him about first getting the news of his Grandad's death he told me:

> My Dad picked me up from school here, then I started to cry on the way home. And when I went to my cousins' (house) they wouldn't tell my cousin all about it because if she found out she'd be very upset. I said to my Aunty, 'You'll have to tell her sometime because she's going to find out anyway'. So she told her and she started crying.

Peter's wisdom about the importance of telling the truth, and his own strategies around death, display a maturity that many deny he possesses. As the pioneering work of Elisabeth Kübler-Ross has shown, children at all levels of health and cognitive ability display a spiritual dimension that sustains and renews them once they completely trust those who give unconditional care.

CHAPTER 9

Strategies for Renewal and Growth

Throughout *Helping Children to Manage Loss* there are personal references that show different factors which have enabled children to work through their experience of loss. However in this chapter we will consider other strategies that those who work with children might find effective. In some cases it will be necessary to work via the parents, other family members, or other professionals. Whatever the link to the child, these strategies can be adapted to suit a variety of situations in which the child who has experienced loss finds himself.

The Importance of Giving Clear Information

Health professionals such as nurses, doctors and emergency service workers may be on the scene when a child is given particularly upsetting news of loss, serious injury/illness or death. However wherever possible the person to whom the child feels closest should generally be the one to break the news. The history of trust, shared experiences and confidence that has built up between the child and this closest adult will provide an important anchor at a time of crisis.

When this is not possible, for instance where both parents have been involved in an accident, then the child should be re-united with a known, loving adult – family member or friend – as soon as possible. This person should then give the news, or where the child already knows, give the news again. Often a child is so shocked when first given such news they find it impossible to grasp what is said, so it is wise to clarify that they understand what has happened. Once the child can accept the reality of the event the mourning process can begin.

Attempts to jolly the child along, or adopting a cheery, 'normalising' approach denies the child the opportunity to respond in their own way. If you provide a model of coping which denies the true import of the event, the child will repress their true reaction under your pressure.

Major illness in childhood as we saw earlier causes great strain to all involved. If a parent has been told that their child has a major disability or a life threatening illness such as cancer, they will probably feel devastated. At the same time there will be enormous pressure to keep control because of the child's vulnerability. In the midst of this turmoil the child has to be told enough to satisfy their immediate needs, which may entail giving very distressing news.

Inside, part of the parent or medical staff may be crying for secrecy, as if by the denial the pain can be closed away, but such denial will not help the child. They need to know as much as they want to and can manage. Children usually will not ask for more than they can take on board, and will ask for more details when and if they feel they can face what the replies will reveal. Children cope better when they can talk openly about their condition and the child's attitude is a pivotal factor in the successful long term psychological and social adjustment.

Easing the pain of children who experience loss is facilitated when it has the bedrock of truth. Lying to children causes all sorts of difficulties, not least that the child may find it impossible to trust in future if they are let down by those on whom they rely.

On receiving bad news the child may feel devastated, shocked, hurt, disbelieving – any range of emotions, as we saw in Chapter 2. As a person supporting the child, you need to show by your balanced, compassionate attitude that you can accept the child's feelings whatever they are. Children are often inhibited and anxious about expressing feelings that are different, and may unwittingly be pushed into expressing only those which are 'allowed'.

If you are present when the news is delivered, or thereafter, ensure they know that you are really there to help in whatever way you can. Actually say, 'I am here, you aren't alone.' If appropriate hold the child, sit them on your knee or sit next to them. Safe touch can reassure and comfort, however do respect any cultural or gender boundaries which may make this inadvisable. The child who feels isolated and abandoned will be reassured by your physical presence.

Following a Death

The words used to inform a child of a death depend on the child's age, level of maturity and their relationship with the dead person. Placing the death in context can be helpful, such as, 'You know your Grandma had been in hospital and that she had to have an operation. Well, because of her age and because she was too frail, she couldn't manage to get better, and she died this morning'. Then it is important to stop. Allow the child to take in the information and let them respond. Relating a person's death to recent events connects the child to what was happening in the past and makes it harder for the child to deny the news, or to deny the impact on their own thoughts and feelings.

When a child receives such news they may cry, ask questions or talk about what they feel. They may seem to be completely unaffected, but do not interpret this as being unconcerned, remember that children have to somehow protect themselves from being overwhelmed. Do not rush them but give them space to react. That will enable you to decide what will be the most helpful action next. Certainly encourage them to talk. If the child talks about changes they had noticed in the deceased person, try to verify the truth or clarify misconceptions where you find them. By doing this you can increase the child's confidence in their own understanding of this new experience.

Young children in particular understand life mainly through their feelings rather than their intellect. Wherever possible link the news to their sensory or bodily awareness. For instance, you might say, 'You probably felt that there was something wrong when your mum came to pick you up at school…', 'I expect that you got the feeling that Grandma wasn't doing too well when there was that telephone call from the hospital,' or 'Sometimes people feel knotted up inside when they are worried and maybe it feels like that to you now. Is that how you feel?'. A caring, sensitive approach with ample time for the child to ask questions, and time for them to be answered honestly in an atmosphere that promises safety and emotional reassurance encourages healing.

For some children pointing out that death is universal and inevitable, with examples from what happens in the rest of nature, can sometimes ease the strain. It can alleviate the feelings of guilt and responsibility that some children feel. Learning that illness and disease, as well as accidents, are unpredictable and unavoidable, is part of the hard work of growing up. Children will have experienced other, minor separations: going to school for the first time, staying away from home overnight, perhaps losing a friend when they moved away. Sometimes it can be helpful to remind the bereaved child of these. They can then recall the event and the feelings and will know, somewhere deep inside, that although it was difficult, they survived. This often reassures a child that they will come through it all, though they cannot consciously acknowledge it yet. Do not trivialise the impact of the present situation though, death is the ultimate separation and they still have to go through the painful process of coming to terms with it.

The Funeral as Rite of Passage

The most important public event that follows a death is the funeral. It is a rite of passage that marks a significant life change, both to those directly affected by the loss and their wider community. For children it can be frightening, comforting, boring or sustaining, so much depends on the reactions of others around them. Many children's fantasies about funerals and cremations are all too frequently inspired by television and video horrors. This means that some children initially need clear, reassuring explanations about what does and does not happen.

A child should be allowed to take part in whatever customary rituals there are according to their cultural tradition. They will get through their grieving more successfully if they know from those around them that it is acceptable to express feelings.

Children I spoke to at the Alder Centre in Liverpool said without exception that they were glad they attended the funeral of their siblings. Thirteen-year-old Andrew explained how he was prepared for his brother's funeral. A good friend of his mother's sat down with him and explained exactly what would happen, what the procedure would be. He felt less anxious because he knew what to expect, where the coffin would be and his needs to be part of the ceremony were respected.

When Sian's husband died in a tragic accident leaving two young children, the short, moving service held in the city crematorium was a great comfort to family and friends alike. In the front pew the children sat on either side of their mother, whilst grandparents and extended family flanked them, a protective family bond strengthening them all. There were no religious references in the service, instead once everyone was seated Sian went to the dais. She spoke of her love for her husband, of the good times and the bad times, of friendships and joys, and read a short poem about what their love meant to her and how that love would sustain her.

Sian's simple, direct tribute was followed by two from very close friends, and between each of these addresses pieces of music that held particular significance for the family were played. The middle one was a lively, country tune, almost a child's nursery song in which the last verse included the idea that death meant 'no longer being alive'. The children could understand the words readily, could identify with the situation and Sian believed it helped them to comprehend the actuality of his death. Throughout the children were a central part of this funeral, not insignificant appendages.

During the short ceremony Kate, the five-year-old girl, looked round smiling at friends and gazing curiously at the strange building in which she found herself. Her seven year old brother Seth, half way through the service began to cry and continued to do so on and off until it finished. There was constant, steady regard for him from his mother and grandfather who at no time tried to prevent him from expressing his sorrow. Finally as everyone gathered outside, Seth's upset was temporarily relieved as he saw two of his old nursery school teachers who had known the family well for five years. Their presence held a continuity and the connection that had supported Seth in the past was supporting him now, and clearly made a huge difference to both children. Very soon Sian took the children home, back to the familiar surroundings where family and close friends stayed with them until the day of their father's funeral was over.

One final point worth mentioning about this exemplary cremation was that as mourners arrived the funeral director distributed cards. These asked for the name, details of the relationship, whether friend or colleague, and gave an opportunity for a message. Later these were collected and passed on to Sian. As there were so many people present and she was still in shock, it was unlikely that Sian would able to remember everyone who attended. The cards gave a physical record that could be kept for the children in the future.

Some weeks later Sian contacted me because she was worried about Kate who was re-enacting the cremation. I assured her that 'playing funerals' is a way that younger children incorporate their new knowledge of death and the rituals that surround it. It can be quite a shock to see a child digging a real or pretend hole and putting a doll in it, meantime saying, 'In you go. Now you're dead'. This play is not a sign of disrespect but the young child's way of taking in what they have experienced. Children learn to integrate and master their life experiences through play, it is part of the child's grief work.

Memory Boxes

Children often want to know, later on, what was thought of their dead parent or sibling, so it is prudent to keep any messages of sympathy. It can be helpful to arrange a meeting for the anniversary of the person's death. Friends may contribute by writing on a postcard their name, when they met the deceased person, and one memory they would like to share. The bereaved child can then keep these and put them in their 'memory box' if they have got one. These physical reminders give great solace that sustain a child through turbulent times of growth and provide a link for future partners and children as yet unknown.

Friends and relatives can write letters to the child, send mementos and so on. This will help redress the balance a little and comfort the child at the time and at points in the future. Children need continuity of loving care, stability and security following loss.

Children like to have a 'piece' of the person they loved – a possession, some linking object – for often children fear they will lose the memory of the person and be totally bereft. They also need to know at an appropriate point that they may forget what their loved person looked like. At the time of death or separation such an idea seems preposterous, but most people struggle to keep an image alive and feel guilty about it. What we tend to recall is the image from a particular photograph, so it can be comforting to keep one on display. Small comforters are reassuring.

Strengthening positive memories of the lost person is one of the kindest things a caring adult can do for the child. This does not mean you start to idealise them or turn them into some kind of plaster saint, it means remembering warts and all but celebrating the good times they had together. Help by celebrating the life as well as mourning the death.

Unconditional Listening

When nine-year-old Malcolm's Grandmother died he felt that people did not help him at all because, 'Everybody thought it was her own fault because she smoked a lot.' This type of judgmental response is the very opposite of unconditional listening. This critical response does not acknowledge or respect the emotions of the person who has sustained the loss and inhibits mourning.

There can be serious consequences if children are not allowed to express their feelings, if they are not listened to. A famous example is that of Charles Darwin. After his mother died when he was eight years old, his father and elder sisters refused to allow him to speak of her, all expression of emotion was frowned upon. Darwin, who rose to great fame for his scientific work described in *The Origin Of The Species* was dogged by ill health throughout his life. In later years he said he could not recall the death of his mother at all. The strict taboo surrounding her death meant that his sorrow was driven deep below the surface into his subconscious. Many believe that his chronic ill health was essentially psychiatric and psychosomatic in origin. The only acceptable release for his pain was through inexplicable suffering himself (Bowlby 1991).

If a child can work through all the grief and pain as early as possible there is less likelihood that he will suffer the same fate as Darwin. Feelings of guilt may be particularly hard for the child to express, but can be seen in a child's behaviour, for instance they may constantly put themself down, say 'I'm stupid', or 'No-one likes me', or 'I'll never be any good at anything.' They may also be morose, lethargic, isolated and/or have lots of aches and pains. These may well indicate that they are bottling up feelings but their behaviour and body language tell you there is something amiss. Unconditional listening takes account of non-verbal communication as much as it does of spoken words.

The 1989 Children Act gave legal recognition to the importance of parenting. It decreed that the courts must make the child's welfare their paramount consideration, above the needs of the parents, grandparents or anyone else involved with the child, when deciding what arrangements for their future are to be. In almost all public law cases the court will appoint a guardian *ad litem* for the child so that the child's rights can be represented and protected. However, parental responsibility is now legally defined and can be given over to the person – grandparent, unmarried father – who the court deems to be the more suitable carer. And the needs and views of the child will outweigh all other claims. At last children have a legal voice in their own future, though that may not be comforting for all parents.

Protection

The greatest need a child has in times of mourning is the need for love, support and companionship. They need to be shielded from too many pressures and not be expected to change suddenly, or to take on new roles too soon. Many children find friends have really helped them through the misery of loss. Some feel freer to express their conflicting emotions with peers and gain support that way. Best friends fend off nosy enquires in playground probing, and intervene with teachers too.

The Support Network

Continuity in school and home routines provide bereaved children with important social support systems that have enormous potential to buffer the impact of loss. Changes in the child's lifestyle and environment at the time of death constitute additional stresses that may jeopardise their ability to master loss. In fact, many child experts believe that it is not the death of a parent that is so destructive for a child's future well-being, but the cumulative effects of all the other changes that may be set in motion and disrupt the whole foundation of the child's life.

Wherever possible those closest to the child should be empowered to give support following loss. Grandparents can have a particularly valuable role to play after a divorce for example. If their marriage is still intact they provide an example of continuity of generations, living proof that relationships can be reliable and enduring. Enlisting the help of grandparents who do not take sides can be crucial in helping the child to maintain feelings of positive self esteem. It shows that relationships can be fulfilling and continuous. Grandparents do not need to live close by to give support, letters and telephone calls as well as occasional visits will be beneficial. The child will enjoy their loving concern especially where it is not coupled with intrusive interference or indiscreet information seeking.

Physical Comfort

Physical comforters give the child solid reminders of care and comfort. They put the child in touch with happier times without this ever being verbalised. For example a hot water bottle in bed may help the child snuggle down and feel cosy even though it may not be cold outside, or if the child is watching television it may reassure and give them something to hold on to. During the day some children who have experienced a loss like extra layers of clothing, they reduce the coldness induced by the shock to the system. These small actions help a child feel especially cared for and layered against the possibility of harm. At bedtime children may feel more assured if they can hear background family talk or soft music. When they hear familiar, comforting sounds they feel less alone and vulnerable.

Respect

Children can be easily offended in the period following a major loss. They react with unusual sensitivity to questions, or imagine injury in harmless remarks. In dealing with a child's heightened vulnerability, firstly make it clear you will look after them. Show you respect their fears even if they seem unreasonable to you. The child should be encouraged to ask for what they want rather than leaving it to others to guess their needs from their behaviour. Teaching a child skills of assertiveness often decreases inappropriate passive or aggressive behaviour.

A child may feign illness because they want a working parent to stay with them. Where the parent cannot agree to the request, it is more helpful to make the hidden agenda visible. For instance the parent might say, 'I know you want me to stay off work and spend the day with you but I can't do that. We can have extra time together as soon as I get home, so we'll do something special then. Just the two of us. OK?' This clarity and negotiation reassures the child that their needs are being taken seriously. The respect for the child helps maintain their feelings of self-worth, a common casualty during periods of loss.

Keep Children Informed

Children need to be given information that is appropriate to their age and level of maturity, and in addition they need to be told of changes which affect their lives. Keeping children informed about what is going on eases strain, for instance where a relationship at home is breaking down, the child may think that the rows or silences are par for the course. Parents assume the child recognises the extent of the discord, but unless the situation is clarified misunderstandings abound. If the decision is to separate for example, then both parents would be advised to tell the child together, otherwise the child may worry about whether the other parent knows what is going on. They may worry about whether they are supposed to talk about it. If both are present it helps the child to know that the decision belongs to both, that it is adult business and that they need not take sides.

Where separation is the loss involved, the parents should explain the reasons for their decision in language that honestly reflects their positions. Fudging and made up excuses will not help in the long term. Intimate details may not be appropriate but the child can be told 'Mummy and Daddy don't love each other in the way we used to and that is making us very unhappy so...' The parents may liken it to the way best friends grow apart and choose other friends. The details are not so important as is the way it is explained, the child needs to know it is not their fault. Divorce is the business of adults not the responsibility of children, and this cannot be emphasised too strongly.

The relationship between parent and child must continue wherever possible, and whilst the parents may want to wipe the slate clean and start all over again, what the child needs is continuity of contact with both parents. In the turmoil of change they need the stability zones that familiar faces and places bring. We all have a basic need for safety, and when we experience loss it touches our deepest fear of abandonment and annihilation. With children this is magnified, which is why it is so important that they be kept informed.

Following Divorce/Separation

What counts for most children following divorce is the quality of the separate relationship with each parent. Anna Coote and her co-authors confirmed earlier findings that within two years of divorce more than one third of children have no contact with the parent who left (Coote 1991). After ten years more than half have lost contact altogether. Strategies to avoid this compounding loss must be sought.

Continued contact needs to be a priority. Children generally find this really important, as Sarah who is now twelve told me:

> When I was three and my brother was eight my Mum and Dad split up because he was always working late. We were allowed to see him at the weekends but we were not allowed to stay overnight. Now my brother is sixteen. He lives with my Dad, his girlfriend and her son. I live with my Mum and Stepdad and I'm allowed to see my Dad and stay overnight now. The thing that helped me get over it was going to see my Dad.

The continued emotional relationship provides security even though physical changes in living arrangement occur, and children who have contact immediately after separation enjoy more regular meetings and have satisfactory relationships for longer with the non-resident parent than those children where there is a gap at the start.

We must bear in mind though that for some children continued contact is neither advisable nor possible. The child may interpret broken contact as a punishment, perhaps because they have been disruptive or difficult. Clear explanations, respect for the child's wishes, and putting the needs of the child first are of paramount importance. Children can get torn apart by their parents' conflict. In the story of Solomon, the real mother is the one who refused to have her baby cut in half.

Conflict Resolution

Most children of divorced parents I have spoken to told me categorically that above all else they detested being 'piggy in the middle' of still warring parents, especially where parents used them as informants about the other's love life or new domestic arrangements. Parents need to reduce stress for their children by the avoidance of denigrating remarks aimed at their ex-partner, nor should they criticise their child when they express warmth towards the other parent. Children retreat and are accused of being miserable when they seek safety in silence.

The post-divorce relationship should be kept civilised by parents being courteous on the telephone, at handovers and other points of contact. Children have told me that they hate the way their divorced parents argue over every small thing. These children do not want to be dragged into bickering about every petty decision. It confuses them, tears them apart, so that often they reject both parents. It is important to empathise.

There is bound to be an element of conflict in the resolution of loss. Encourage the child to face the conflicting drives to hold on to what has gone and at the same time let go and move on. It is a pull between the past and the future, the known and the unknown. It is a keynote to griefwork and can be seen in the grieving child's craving to be alone yet seeking company; avoiding reminders from the past yet constantly referring to it. As you work with the child you may experience this conflict directly in hostility vented towards you. The child perhaps sees your help as something that will make them leave the past behind when part of them may not be ready to do so. You are the object of hostility and a source of support.

Working through this conflict is an essential part of the process. It will not be hurried and the greater the loss, the more difficult it may be. However, healing is taking place even as they hurt. As people who wish to play a part in the healing process, we have to accept that whilst we can validate the child's feelings we cannot stop their pain.

Ways in which we help ease the pain of loss are woven into everyday life. Helping the child develop self-confidence for example, is a key factor in overcoming loss of any kind. If the child feels positive about themself they can usually seek help from other trusted adults outside the home – grandparents, neighbours, teachers or friends – when they are distressed about family events or when that customary support has ceased for whatever reason. Fear and self-blame may cause a child's self-belief to be sorely tried so they will need affirmation to build and keep up self-esteem. The child who is valued will learn to value themself.

In the final analysis children who experience loss have to accept the most difficult thing of all – the pain of truth – that their parents will not get back together; that their dead mother will not come back home again; that living is unpredictable and uncertain. They have to learn that their dearly held magical fantasy of a happy united family will not now exist, no matter how good or helpful they are. Plea bargaining does not usually help when the worst has happened. The paradox is that the ultimate test of the child's strength is their ability to accept their powerlessness. If they can do this, especially where they are in the care of trusted adults, they will come through with great self-awareness and depth. Life will never be the same, but hopefully they will be able to enjoy it despite early loss.

Healthy mourning is achieved when a person accepts changes in their external life, makes corresponding changes in their internal life, and finally makes the necessary reorientation to feel closeness and attachment once more. It means learning to say 'Good-bye' and being able at a future point, to say 'Hello'. With healthy mourning there is a sense of growth through suffering and grief. Many believe the experience of loss to be a valuable learning process, and later in life feel that it opened them to greater depths of love and a deeper appreciation of life.

But still I can hear some of you say, 'How can I reply when I'm asked by parents, 'Will anything really help my child recover?' You may find the following passage helpful. It is not a formula to be adopted wholesale, but an approach which can be adapted to fit the people and circumstances of each situation.

To a Parent

Caught up in the desperate undertow of grief, when you feel that you are being dragged down deeper and deeper, where it feels you will never rise for air again, never get back to a safe land you have known, it is difficult to accept that recovery is possible.

Strategies to Ease the Pain of Loss
Some thoughts to share

The loss of a major figure in the life of a child may take a child years to get over. Some children, like some adults, may find that this most painful experience of their lives is one which irrevocably changes them. There are extreme cases of unresolved mourning but in the majority of cases children go through a healthy mourning period and come out the other side, often as stronger more compassionate individuals. Maybe these thoughts will help you to remember what you *can do* especially in those bleak moments when you seem to lose all hope:

I Can...

recognise the loss and validate my child's experience by saying so.

be there to listen if my child wants to talk.

reassure my child that strong feelings, from rage to despair, are a normal part of grieving, and that to express them is healthier than keeping them bottled up.

be honest.

show I care by having time to be with my child when they need me.

accept that children need a caring, consistent, trustworthy adult to be there. If I cannot do it because I am too wrapped up in my own grief, then it is OK to find a friend or relative that I trust to stand in for me.

accept that we can grieve together as a family so that my children can see that the pain of loss is part of life. It is natural. It is not something to be ashamed of or hidden.

give comfort by keeping to familiar surroundings and predictable routines.

involve my children in practical tasks and decisions. There is so much to do after a death and my children may have no concept of what these tasks are. Allowing my child to be part of the process will help dispel feelings of powerlessness. It will enable them to see that they are not totally isolated – death happens to other people too, and they have to go through similar activities.

remember that if my child has cause to grieve they must grieve. There are no easy short cuts but I can give my support.

empathise. I need not say 'I know exactly what you are feeling' because I'm not them and I cannot know exactly. I can feel with them but I have to respect them as a separate person to me, and accept that their feelings might be very different from mine.

if everything else seems to have failed, and my child seems stuck in their grief, I can refer them for professional help through their school or via the GP. That is not failure, but being a caring parent.

Eventually my child might still feel sorrow but hopefully the pain will not be so raw, and we can build on what we have together and the positive memories we share.

CHAPTER 10

School Strategies for Renewal 1

I was homesick during the whole of my first term at St. Peter's. Homesickness is a bit like seasickness. You don't know how awful it is till you get it, and when you do, it hits you right in the top of your stomach and you want to die. The only comfort is that both homesickness and seasickness are instantly curable. The first goes away the moment you walk out of the school grounds and the second is forgotten as soon as the ship enters port.

(Dahl 1986)

Every school community will suffer loss, including bereavement, from time to time. The school itself may be both a source of loss for pupils through academic failure, bullying or staff turnover or bereavement, and school may be the place where feelings about other losses are expressed. These experiences impact on the life of the school and individual performances within it. In fact as families become less cohesive, teachers may be the child's best opportunity to find help, since they probably have more regular, consistent contact than anyone else.

There is a strong body of evidence which shows that stressful life changes have considerable implications for the overall physical and emotional well-being of the pupils, their adjustment and their academic achievements. This obviously plays a significant part in their subsequent school career. At its simplest level anxiety reduces attention span, increases distractibility, lowers efficiency and may cause fear of failure and actual failure in academic performance. (Varma 1993)

For children whose lives are affected by abuse, bereavement, divorce, drug related problems, broken relationships or any of the other manifest miseries in our society, school may be a safe haven in a frightening world. As a teacher, with all the demands of the National Curriculum and the pressures of meeting the academic needs of pupils, you still have to cope with the emotional lives of the children in your class, whatever their age. Knowing how loss affects them will increase your ability to help them survive the trauma.

Bereavement

We will consider bereavement first. Today in Britain we have less direct experience of mortality than at any other time in our history. Children used to recognise that death was part of the cycle of life, but as that is no longer the case there is a strong argument for putting death on the curriculum. Change is part of life and with every loss there is the potential for growth and gain, an aspect of death often overlooked. We teach the facts of life in school, but what of the facts of death? Inevitably the school staff and fellow pupils must respond to the pupils who return to school following bereavement, but what can they do?

Ann, a head teacher, had to tell her staff and pupils that eleven-year-old Mark who had gone home from school at lunch time would not be returning. On his way home he was knocked down by a car and at 1.00pm she was told that he was unlikely to survive. She gathered the pupils together after all the staff had been informed, and at three o'clock passed on the news that the boy they played with that morning had died. There were tears and lots of questions which were answered simply and sensitively. A letter was prepared to accompany each child home that night, so that families knew of the event and what had taken place at school.

At Mark's parents' request the funeral cortege stopped outside the school gates on the way to a private family funeral later in the week, and the children stood at the school fence to say their goodbyes. Nobody asked the children to remain silent but they did. Everyone was moved by the dignity and quietness of the moment as the children stood and watched. Later they returned to a subdued afternoon's schooling, where gentle, quiet activities were the order of the day.

Teachers at the school told me that questions about what would happen to Mark went on for many, many months. They asked what would happen to the coffin, what would happen to his body, and so on. Whilst some staff found this quite morbid, they understood the pupils need to come to terms with his death. They wanted to understand this new experience. Two years later the children appear to have got over Mark's death. They sometimes point him out in the under elevens 'Hall of Fame' football team photographs and remember times together, but it is part of their shared history now and the grieving has stopped.

When I was in Northern Ireland making a television film about children's dreams, the headmistress of a primary school in the heart of Belfast explained how her pupils coped with grief. Almost every child in the school had a member of their family who had been either killed or injured in the 'troubles'.

Throughout the years the school offered a place of normality, continuity and relative safety in a disordered world. The close knit bonds between parents, cousins, aunts, uncles and grandparents meant that hurt was widespread when any in the family were affected. 'The thing that makes the greatest difference as to whether a child copes well or badly following a death,' she said, 'is the way the child's mother copes. If she can grieve but carry on caring for the children, then somehow they manage and carry on with their lives.' All the research literature I have come across backs up her belief.

Her school, like so many in Northern Ireland, played an integral part in the community whenever there was a death. The head teacher or her deputy would visit the child's home as soon as news reached them that a member of any of their pupils' family had been taken seriously ill or had died. It made no difference if it was at the weekend when the news came, the tight-knit community expected and respected the fact that the teachers had a caring concern about more than the academic needs of their pupils, and would be actively involved at times of need. Indeed, seeing this continuity between home and school allowed children affected by grief to feel more secure and less anxious about having to explain about the death when they next attended school.

Some bereaved children may want to get back to school as soon as possible for a whole variety of reasons. One may be because having been bereaved they become special, a star because something unusual has happened in their family. Rene Magritte, the painter, whose mother committed suicide when he was thirteen, remembered little of his feelings at that time except 'a certain pride at being the centre of attention in a drama.' This novelty value will for some children be a treat. The sadness, anger, pain and guilt get mixed up with the nice feelings that are engendered by teachers and pupils being especially kind to them. The child may want to get back to school because perhaps there will be a special assembly which they want to attend. However, whilst being famous for five minutes takes their mind off the trauma of the bereavement, the need for space will probably come later.

John found that school and his school work routine was a welcome relief in the period following his sister's death. 'I wanted the teachers to know but then leave it', he told me, 'I didn't want to talk about it.' Talking was too difficult. He pointed out one aspect of bereavement which is easily overlooked. 'Finding the right words,' he said, 'that's what's hard. Do I say I have one sister because only one is alive, or do I say two? And if they ask questions, eventually I have to say that she's dead and...' His words trailed off, emphasising his feelings that there was not an easy solution.

Another twelve-year-old described a French lesson at school which was about the family. 'We were writing an essay. I was so upset suddenly, that I just had to walk out. I was crying. I didn't know if I was an only child or if I had a brother. But he was dead.' Like John he felt that if he said his brother was dead he would be constantly pushed into explaining all about his death. Bereaved children must re-establish a self-identity, for 'Who am I?' becomes a major concern. One element for Alan is 'Am I an only child? Who am I?' He needed help in his search.

Helping children cope with the aftermath of loss can come down to very simple aspects, such as communication skills. Knowing the words to say it and then how to stop uncomfortable questioning will ease the child's stress. John might say, 'I had two sisters but X died' or, 'I have one sister alive.' Alan might say 'I'm an only child now but I used to have a brother.' And in response to the likely question, 'What happened to him?' He can say, 'I don't like to talk about it' or 'I don't talk about X because it upsets me.' Helping children behave assertively in this way will increase their confidence and enable them to decide when and with whom they talk about their loss.

Boys may find the expectations of others, especially their peers, hamper any expression of tender feeling. As John told me, 'In an all-boys school you can't let them see you are down, otherwise they'll take advantage of you. Inside you are all emotional but you can't let them see.'

Divorce and Separation

The loss of a parent through separation or divorce is potentially more disturbing than losing a parent through death. Death is final but divorce leaves the child's loss unresolved and ongoing. The child grieves but there is no recognised ritual such as burial to mark the end of that part of their life. The pupil continues to attend school whilst an emotional storm rages round them. School may well be a safe place which acts as a 'stability zone' where the security offered allows the individual to recharge their emotional batteries without suffering undue pressure. For some children it is a particular teacher or place in school that acts as the anchor, for others it is the whole place. This needs to be taken into account when changes in groups or routines are made. Where possible any significant changes should be delayed until the child's life is more settled.

The disruption to home life is likely to be severe enough to impair educational performance to some degree, and may in extreme cases require specific intervention. It is useful to bear in mind that divorce is a process, not a single discrete event. Recent research by Dr Kathleen Kiernan at the Family Policy Study Centre highlights this, showing as it does that children from broken homes might suffer learning difficulties long before their parents separate publicly (Kiernan 1991). Whether performance at school suffers long term depends on the nature and quality of the revised family arrangements and the new psychological climate. So, the ultimate outcome of the child's well-being depends not just on what has been lost, but on what has been created in its place.

Anya, whose parents had a bitter divorce, had an unspoken fear that her father would kidnap her from school one day. She developed all sorts of avoidance ploys until her baffled mother finally unearthed the reason. She was visibly less anxious after her mother spoke to school staff and arranged for her to be picked up from the classroom rather than at the school gate. For some time Anya had insisted her mother accompany her to her friend's house down the street, instead of going alone as she had prior to the separation. If she had no 'guard' she would stay at home. Such additional security may be inconvenient for the adults involved but these small acts of reassurance give clear signals to the child that she is cared for and will be protected. Anya soon regained her confidence and was able to put her fears in perspective. She needed time and recognition of her stress in order to cope effectively.

Though children may share the same age, there may be huge differences in their physical and emotional maturity. Bearing this in mind, it may be useful to have the following age framework for understanding children's reactions to death:

Between three- to five-years-old death seems like sleep, or going on a long journey. The child believes the dead person can wake up or come back later. From five to nine years the reality of death is understood but children have difficulty imagining that anyone they love, or they themselves, might die. Usually by the age of nine the irreversibility of death is understood and whilst adolescents may regress to earlier stages, they like adults may be preoccupied with the meaning of death.

Developmental differences are reflected in the way children respond to loss. Certain emotions become more controlled and concealed as children grow and learn about what is acceptable/normal in our society. If we start with children at nursery school you can see the expression of raw feeling. David's nursery school teacher described his reaction to the absence of his father:

David is a three year old child who is very aggressive towards his peers and adults. Intellectually he is very bright and enjoys all activities, but he can suddenly switch and become very violent. He directs most of his aggression towards his teacher – me! I feel this is because he knows that whatever he does I will still love him. This does put a strain on me and I have to try very hard to keep providing positive warmth. I worry because he seems so miserable and unhappy… I've talked to other members of staff as well as his Mum who seems loving and caring towards him. If I see a situation where I feel he may harm himself or another person I try to avert it and guide him on to something else.

This anti-social acting-out behaviour is typical of a young child who doesn't have the confidence or verbal skills to fully explain their anger and grief. A teacher less skilled than Helen might be tempted to deal with David by punishing him. Punishment may curtail the behaviour at the time but it drives all those feelings below the surface, where they rumble away only to erupt at unforeseen points in the future. Whilst the child has to be stopped to prevent them hurting themself and/or others, punishment is no long-term solution.

Helen's firm handling is therapeutic. It recognises David's needs as he mourns the loss of his father, and responds to them sympathetically without losing sight of the fact that he still requires consistent boundaries. His anger, displaced onto people and things in the nursery, is guided away from aggressive encounters. He is given every opportunity to play in water, sand and clay as a creative outlet, and because Helen has found music to be most soothing for him, she has ensured regular dance and movement sessions with the whole group. This maintains David's positive connection to the whole group and provides an important feeling of belonging. This is essential because his tantrums make him something of an isolate. She tries to involve him in small groups, and by basic social skills training as well as therapeutic play and listening, Helen has helped him to integrate with his peers more successfully.

Young children like David whose development has been delayed or regressed because of trauma, often do well if placed in a small group where they can be given appropriate stimulation and support. They do not do as well if they are in a large group where there is a lot of unstructured, unsupervised activity. This overwhelms their already fragile boundaries and they relieve the tension by exploding physically or verbally. Caring guidance, support and the provision of a stable classroom situation with firm, fair discipline and considerate members of staff, help contain the aggressively acting out child until he has regained or learned personal boundary control.

Suzie, aged five became much more fearful after her parents divorce and this manifested itself in school as well at home. When her mother had to go into hospital Suzie became extremely anxious, though she had not been perturbed by her mother's regular visits for treatment previously. At school Suzie was distressed if there were loud noises or shouting or whenever children were arguing. 'She seems to cower and then kind of freezes, staring, though it isn't as if she is looking at anything,' said her teacher.

All the time Suzie tries to be the perfect little girl. She is still at the 'bargaining' stage of magical belief and thinks that if she is very good her mother will not get sick and her parents will get back together. She told me she was afraid of loud noises, arguments and shouting because, 'bad things would happen, like after Mummy and Daddy shouted and argued, my Daddy went away.' Loud voices in her mind were associated with abandonment.

Children in nursery and infant schools may become much more clingy, fretful and sad in school. Often more demanding, they hold onto security objects such as blankets or special toys, and complain bitterly when having to part from a parent at the start of the school day. Older children when under severe strain may have increased difficulties in school, which may include aggressive disruptive behaviour, stealing, temper tantrums, increased attention seeking and irritability. They are quick to take offence, and subject to mood swings. Events which they would have taken in their stride in the past become major issues and crying with frustration and anger more frequent. This is more likely to happen to the child who is prevented from expressing emotion at home. The child discharges their frustration in another setting, often the school. This unconscious behaviour, known as displacement, can cause all sorts of anxieties for the child, who feels they have no control over their outbursts or their overwhelming emotions. It is frightening for the pupil too, though rarely admitted.

Boys of six to eight whose parents divorce have a particularly difficult time adjusting. Frequently they cannot concentrate in school, fight all and sundry, or withdraw into their own isolated world. Socially and academically they are prone to setbacks. At this age children express powerful yearnings for the absent parent, usually the father, and may idealise him. Whilst idealisation may take place at any age it seems particularly pronounced at this age.

Part of this intense impact on boys is because they are just at the stage where they are developing strong identification with the male role represented by the father, and discovering more clearly their own masculinity. Being left in the mother's care, especially where there are sisters but no brothers, creates all sorts of internal psychological conflicts which the son has to resolve. Continued regular contact with father wherever possible helps, or another trusted male role model needs to be found – uncles, teachers, neighbours; very often the boy will find his own. If it is you the teacher who is singled out, do not be alarmed by the child's dependency on you. Handled carefully it could be an emotional life saver for the child.

Answering Pupils' Questions

Sometimes the questions children ask can be shocking. A six-year-old, on the death of a grandparent, asked 'Are bodies meat?' On the reply, she continued 'Well, why don't we eat the meat instead of putting it in the ground to rot?' This caused some consternation, but highlights the way some children will react to death in a very matter of fact way which can appear cold. There is no correct way to react to death and we must respond to a child's questions openly and honestly.

One teacher commented to me that when a seven-year-old's grandfather died, he asked her what happened to the coffin and the dead body. His mother had told that him that granddad would go to heaven but he was quizzical about this. What he wanted to know was what happened to all the coffins, he accepted the idea of heaven but was worried about the coffins. In school he did a drawing in which he attempted to fit coffins neatly together in that heavenly place. He was trying to logically understand what happened after death and it did not all fit together in his fastidious mind. When the teacher explained that the coffin and the body would decay over time that seemed to satisfy him. He could accept that some other part of his grandfather could go to heaven and so he was released from the worry of sorting it all out in logically.

Teachers who are seen as honest and reliable find pupils will confide about their worries and confessions, which almost always contain some reference to loss. Answers need to be truthful, pitched at the appropriate level, and need to allow for uncertainties. Sometimes people are given information in such an emphatic way that it leaves no room for uncertainty. Even if a person has been diagnosed with a terminal illness for example, and given only weeks to live, no one can give an absolute assurance that the death will take place at the prescribed time. Life always holds uncertainty, and hope is never utterly irrelevant. Work being done in the field of psychoneuroimmunology for instance, shows how hope and the power of self-healing can dramatically influence recovery from illness (Martin 1997). We should be conscious of the effect of our answers, and ensure that they do not rule out hope that something positive will come out of the situation, however bleak it may appear.

In answering questions do not fudge the issue. If you do, the child will probably fantasise the worst response and feel heightened anxiety. They will also feel worse because they pick up on your embarrassment. Should they go ahead and use you as a counsellor and confidante, be prepared for a negative reaction later. Sometime after the event the child may feel embarrassed about their personal revelations and seek to distance themself from them by avoiding you.

Life-Threatening Illness

Children who have life-threatening illnesses may still attend school whenever their health and treatment programmes allow, and the school community can play a vital part in enabling such children to lead a life outside their family home and hospital. Jason, aged eight when he died, struggled to get to school whenever he could, as his teacher explained:

> Jason changed from a sturdy, rebellious, loving little boy, to a shrunken skeletal shadow. He was a good-natured child though towards the end of his life he was in tremendous pain. When he first started the treatment he came into school and tried very hard to do his lessons though it was difficult for him. He was upset and unhappy when he lost all his hair, and he asked his Mum to get him a woolly bobble hat. He wore it continually at first, only taking it off to go swimming which he loved and when he was in his own classroom amongst all his friends. Jason kept on coming to school and wanted so much to come. Towards the end the caretaker would push him across in his buggy. He would join in if he could, or doze in a put-up bed in the Wendy House.
>
> Jason knew he was poorly, in fact he was aware that he was very poorly, but right up until the last time I saw him he would try to smile. He was an incredibly brave and courageous child.

The staff of this primary school kept every avenue open for Jason and his family to maintain close links. His younger sister went to the nursery there too. His classmates were tolerant and patient when his illness made him snappy and moody, and they seemed to form a protective ring round him. His teacher felt all the children had become much more sensitive and caring because of their experience of Jason's illness and subsequent death.

After Jason died the school held a collection for a wreath and the head teacher and class teacher attended the funeral with the caretaker. The school now has two trophies in memory of Jason named after him. Both are for swimming. Jason loved swimming and up until he was very ill and weak he would go swimming with his class every week. The trophies are awarded annually to an infant and junior school child, not to the child who is the best swimmer but to the one who has, against all the odds, persevered and made the most progress.

Maggie, Jason's teacher, found that the experience of working with and becoming closer to Jason and his family very enriching, though not without its painful side:

Parts of the relationship I found very stressful, like watching Jason deteriorating, listening to his Mum telling me about the drug treatment they were giving him and how much better he would get...while the school nurse was shaking her head and saying privately that the prognosis wasn't very hopeful. I never told Cathy (Jason's Mum) because I didn't think it would serve any useful purpose. I think deep down she knew what would happen but pretending helped dull the pain. The most stressful occasion was going to the cancer centre to see Jason. I went one hot, clammy, heavy day after school. I wasn't looking forward to it. Although it was a children's ward it was bleak and bare and the windows were barred. There were two rows of beds with about six or seven children in, from about three months to ten years and they all had one thing in common besides the tumours: felt-tip pen lines and crosses on their bald heads where they were to have their radiation treatment...it's a memory that will stay with me for a long time to come.

If you show that you care about a child suffering the trauma of loss, others, pupils and parents alike get the message that you are a person who can be trusted and they will seek out your empathic support.

Childhood Abuse

An area of particular concern to teachers is the whole range of abuse that children suffer and whilst chapter seven covers abuse in its widest sense, this section is concerned with implications for schools.

Surveys carried out in Britain and America tell us that one in ten children has suffered abuse. This is a conservative estimate, many would put the figure much higher, so in any classroom you are likely to come across children who have been abused. In a course on assertiveness in the workplace I ran recently, four women out of twelve spoke of childhood abuse, including incest, violence, and sexual molestation by a school teacher in the primary school. In two instances these women had not spoken of the abuse before, because just like children, they felt scared they would not be believed or that they would be judged as somehow being to blame, because that is what abusers tell their victims.

Children may attempt to tell you of abuse in their writing or in the pictures they draw. These are forms of communication that the child can initiate when words fail. We need to be sensitive enough to recognise when this is happening, even though such revelations may be very disturbing for the adult, in fact so disturbing that we may be tempted to try to block out what is being said, tempted to avoid that truth because it is too hard to bear. Denial and avoidance of 'upset' or 'bother' can be done by pushing the whole issue under the carpet. It may get you off the hook but what will happen to the child? It is not unusual to get a sinking feeling of fear, disbelief or disgust when abuse is disclosed. Some teachers fear that they may be stigmatised if they reveal a case of abuse. If you are the one the child chooses to tell you may feel a sense of inner desolation and dread which often mirrors the feelings of the child who is telling you.

Esther Rantzen, founder of ChildLine, quoted a letter from a girl who had tried to tell a teacher of her abuse, writing it down seemed easier:

> The teacher read my essay and said I had a filthy imagination. My teacher made me stand up in school assembly and said I was a liar and a troublemaker. I never told anyone again, although my stepfather never left me alone. I thought it was my fault and that everyone disliked me. My happiest time was when I had a kidney complaint and went to hospital. I lived in fear of being alone with my stepfather (Rantzen 1986).

Kidscape and other national organisations concerned about the protection of children against sexual assault recognise that many adults find child abuse impossible to believe. They advocate that a child tells one adult after another until eventually believed.

This denial of abuse is unfortunately quite common. Parents too, in warning of the dangers of abuse, find it extremely difficult to tell a child that he or she could be abused by someone they know. Warning about strangers is much easier, yet eighty per cent of victims do know the perpetrator (Rush 1980). Tragically the more the child loves and trusts the adult, the more easily that child can be victimised and persuaded to keep it a secret for a long, long time.

Most studies indicate that one fourth of child victims are first abused before the age of eight, with the peak occurring between the ages of nine and eleven. The profound effect of abuse is too well documented to develop here, there is extensive literature on the subject to follow up. However, when helping children in school it is vital to understand that once the abuse has finished it does not mean that it is all over for the pupil. It is vital not to deny the trauma suffered, nor the long term distress it can cause.

It is the unequal power relationship between adults and children that makes it very difficult for a child to say 'No' to a perpetrator of abuse, particularly where threats and emotional manipulation makes the child increasingly vulnerable and isolated. Personal and social education programmes may for the first time inform children that they have the right to control what other people do to them no matter what the relationship, and this includes those children who have disabilities (O'Day 1983).

If a child discloses abuse to you listen to the child, believe them and give the opportunity for them to talk without overloading them with your condemnation of the perpetrator. The pupil may have conflicting feelings about the abuser, the classic love/hate dilemma. The people you hate outright cause you less conflict than those you sometimes hate and sometimes love. If you can support the child by making sure they know it is not their fault and encourage them to express their feelings it will be more helpful than encouraging the expression of only those feelings which you find acceptable. Listen, show care and empathy, but do not ask leading questions, and if you do not have the required skills, gain expert support for the child.

All people who work with children are by law required to report suspected cases of physical or sexual abuse, and every school should have a designated member of staff trained in child protection. Your organisation will have guidelines as to procedures concerning child abuse, and if you are not sure what they contain you should make yourself familiar with them immediately. Signs of abuse are numerous, ranging from the obviously physical, (such as a child of five on the 'At risk' register who turned up at school with a 'love bite' on his neck given by his father when they were playing 'their game') to the behavioural signs such as nightmares, anxiety and/or isolation, increased aggressive outbursts, and precocious sexual activity as described in Chapter 7.

Many of the signs we have seen in reaction to loss are here too, as well as increased fear of certain adults. However, though these signs might be apparent, it is clearly not acceptable to jump to conclusions about what is happening in a child's life. Instead be ready to listen to the child and if there are a whole range of worrying signs, small when taken individually but significant when put together, then talk to a senior member of staff or discuss it with someone who has expertise in the areas of child sexual abuse. Also, long term confidence in your own ability will be increased by attending training courses organised by the NSPCC or your LEA.

Increased awareness through the media and services such as ChildLine and Kidscape, who also run a programme of information training for teachers and educational events for children in schools, have highlighted anti-victimisation programmes. These stress that children have the right to say 'No', should try to get away from any would-be assailant and should tell someone they trust as soon as possible. Teachers are named as someone to be trusted, and so at such times it is to you that the child will turn.

Beware the Beaming Uncle Bertie and Smiling Auntie Sarah is a play performed for schools by Bedfordshire's Arena Touring theatre. The play reinforces the message that children have the right to repel advances be they amorous or threatening, and helps them to identify responsible adults they might seek out if they are frightened or bewildered. It has provoked a number of disclosures of abuse in the schools where it has been performed. The play was followed up in personal and social education (PSE) lessons, and any child who chose could opt for private counselling by the most appropriate member of staff. The acting company met with staff beforehand to discuss the nature of the play, and described reactions in schools in which they had previously performed, thus enabling the teachers to prepare for possible responses. Information and leaflets from such projects as ChildLine and Incest Survivors were also available, as well as suggestions as to how the themes could be developed back in the classroom.

This kind of direct approach. albeit dramatically couched, gives any abused child the chance to realise they are not on their own and that there are ways out of their situation. Even if they decide not to tell anyone they can understand that there may be a way out in future, should they feel strong enough to take it. Telephone helplines such as ChildLine have provided such support lines to thousands upon thousands of children. In 1991 an experimental helpline for boarding school children was set up after public concern came to a head when the principal of a school was jailed for 10 years for sexual offences against boys. The telephone counsellors received 10,000 calls, mainly about abuse, bullying and distress at being away from home. Though the need was clearly there for a continued helpline the funds were not, and those children will have to join the ranks of others who feel they have nowhere else to turn but an anonymous, caring voice on the other end of a telephone.

UNICEF, the United Nations Children's Fund, brought out a report in 1991 called *The State of the World's Children* (UNICEF 1991). In it children said what they hated about school was being disregarded by teachers, not being listened to and being the subject of teacher abuse. The destructive comments of verbally adept, cruel teachers, have lifelong repercussions as I know only too well from my work with children and adults alike. Those stinging barbs wound deeply, and Gina's experience has always stayed with her. She said:

> Someone in the classroom had not made it to the loo, the turd fell next to my desk. The teacher automatically thought it was me. She insulted me and poured out a mountain of verbal abuse, then she made me sit on the toilet for an hour. The teacher should not have done this to anyone, not even the culprit. I was six years old.

Not all abuse is physical or sexual, though racial abuse may contain both. Ethnic minority group members are all too frequently harassed and victimised. Sima, a fourteen-year-old Asian girl's experience was far from uncommon. Gangs of children in her street used to harass the children because of their colour and their clothes. She told me, 'It was an "us and them" situation and I couldn't tell my parents. I suppose I was being protective towards them.'

Victimisation happens outside the school, in the home, on the street, it can happen anywhere. The distressed child in school may be harbouring secrets that paralyse them with fear and it might be happening to very young children too as Jan remembered: 'When I was about four we used to stay at aunty's. Everytime we were alone my cousin Colin locked me in a cupboard. He threatened to bury me in the garden.' Home-school conflict, as well as intra-family conflict, may explain much under-achievement. It certainly affected Tom's performance: 'My father used to criticise me constantly while I was doing my homework. Said I was lazy. He saw no use in education even though I was very good at school. It was a constant struggle being torn between him and the school teachers.'

Other parents may undermine their children by direct, vicious criticism. One of the cruellest examples I have come across was when I met Lorna, a participant on a training course I was running. She told me why she thought she lacked confidence. Her father, she said was charming and delightful but in drink he became violent and demonic. One day she brought news home that she had failed her 11+. Her father made a cardboard sign on which were printed in large letters the words 'I am a failure', hung it round her neck and sent her to walk up and down the street until he told her she was allowed back in the house. To this day Lorna still lacks any firm belief in her abilities, though she holds a responsible management post which requires intelligence, ability and quick thinking.

Bullying

Bullying, which is what Sima experienced, affects over 1.5 million children in the UK today. Many bullies hurt their victims by name calling, threatening them or demanding money or possessions. Usually the bullies will pick up something about the victim that is different – their clothes, their colour or because they are cleverer – whatever the difference they are mocked and life can be made unbearable, as Katy's was:

> At primary school the other girls in my class would make fun of me because I had a lisp. They would ask me to say 'sausages' and other words starting with 's'. This made me fell so upset and I found myself making excuses and told them I had a brace on my teeth. Eventually I told my mum and she took me to a speech therapist who sorted out my problem. But the misery still haunts me.

Katy was fortunate because her mother listened and took her daughter seriously. Some victims are bulled for so long and so viciously that they believe that they deserve the bullying, keeping their fears secret does not help. If pupils talk of being bullied it is vital that is taken seriously, investigated and prompt remedial action taken. Children have the right to have their concerns taken seriously. When no action is taken the bullied child may employ more self-destructive solutions such as truanting or self-injury.

Our children are victimised more frequently and in many more ways than we realise. The Centre for Criminology at Edinburgh University, in its study on youth, crime and policing, (Interim Report 1992) showed that half of the children in its survey had been the victims of theft, assault or threatening behaviour, and not just in inner city deprived areas. Harassment was reported in all forms from all ages, with bullying as a central anxiety for a high proportion of children. Despite the high level of crime children preferred to deal with the situation themselves, because they feared that adults would not believe them and would turn on them instead, and because they did not want their freedom curtailed.

Many who were not victims were witnesses and were affected by that. They dealt with their experiences by talking to others in the same age group, at least friends understood and were not judgmental. They also stayed around in groups on the streets because it felt safer.

Pete recalled that a boy in his class was systematically bullied by four others but there was a conspiracy of silence between the rest of the class. Eventually there was a show-down he said, and everyone finally admitted what they had seen, but the impact on him was significant. Day in day out for over two years he witnessed the bullying and felt fear that it might happen to him, yet felt guilt that he was doing nothing to stop it. He felt purged by the show-down and grateful that it put an end to the victimisation. He remembered another incident from when he was about fifteen years old, when he was walking back from a concert with some friends. Suddenly out of the blue a gang of lads attacked the black member of his group, the rest kept on walking. Though the adrenaline pumped round and he was very afraid it was all over so quickly he had not time to think, but on reflection feels bad that they all did not fight back.

There are no innocent bystanders in bullying. If you witness an attack and do nothing to help then you collude with the bully. Pete has gained from these experiences to the extent that despite living on the borders of a very troubled area of the city, he has learned to recognise and avoid aggressive situations.

Anyone who reports being bullied should be assured that action will be taken. If it is appropriate the child should keep a diary of dates, incidents, places and times of any bullying. Incidents can be checked more easily where they are monitored. Bullying happens everywhere and the school has an obligation to act *in loco parentis* and if they are not protecting the child then they are failing in their statutory obligation. If parents are still not satisfied with the response they get after making a complaint about bullying they should contact the Board of Governors, who are legally bound to follow up any complaints. If bullying is neglected, allowed to go unchecked in the vain hope that it will go away, it may well escalate. It can blight a child's life by leading to poor performance, truancy, illness – physical and psychosomatic – and even suicide.

The ABC (Anti-Bullying Campaign) was founded in memory of Mark Perry, a thirteen-year-old boy from Oxford who was being bullied at school. One day, attempting to escape his pursuers in the street, he ran into the path of an oncoming van and was killed. ABC provides training, advise and information for anyone concerned about bullying. New initiatives on peer group support systems in schools is having a good deal of success in reducing the incidence of bullying.

Peer group support works on the principal that it is good to talk and recognises that young people are highly dependent on the opinions and support of their peers. Older pupils within a school are given some training in basic counselling and interpersonal skills, and their names and pictures are displayed so that any pupil who feels the need for support can choose someone to talk to confidentially. Of course, the scheme is backed up by careful vetting and support for the pupil 'counsellor', but it offers a first line of help for those young people who find it difficult to confide in adults. In Britain The Prince's Trust has funded the development and evaluation of peer support schemes and we may see much more of this strategy in the future.

Where a child reveals they are being bullied it is helpful to encourage them to think about strategies they could use either to prevent it happening again or to identify methods they could use to tackle the situation. Of course, if the bullying is too threatening or unmanageable then asking the child what they want you to do, or explaining what action you will take, needs to be a priority. Swift protection and intervention must be the way forward, with close monitoring of the situation following whatever action has been taken.

The effects of bullying do not stop there. Frequently the child at the receiving end has suffered a huge blow to their self-esteem so work may be necessary to help them identify the things they like about themself, and the skills they have, so that strategies can be devised to help them feel better about themself and build or re-build friendship. Bullying also has a place on the curriculum, as part of the social and emotional education of pupils. Class discussions can be particularly useful in airing issues in a general way without highlighting individual cases.

One boy explained that bullying others was the only thing that he was good at. It made him feel important because he felt useless at everything at school. He stopped when he changed schools because his new teachers did not make him feel stupid like the old ones, and he did not need to prove himself. It is hard to keep in mind that most bullies are unhappy in some way. Behind the bully is usually a terrified, vulnerable child who is stuck in a destructive cycle of abuse; for the good of all concerned the has to be helped to find other ways to face his difficulties.

A Short Summary of Strategies to Use with Children Suffering Loss

1. Use age-appropriate language and methods of comfort.

2. Be aware of the child's personal attitude towards divorce or death, and any cultural or religious beliefs they may have. Respect the importance of these.

3. Listen to what the child has to say about their experiences and give them the opportunity to express them openly.

4. Use 'small death' such as the death of a classroom pet to help children understand the concept of death.

5. Be sensitive to delayed or subtle grief responses and give room for grief to be expressed.

6. Provide reassurance, continuity and care.

7. If necessary help parents to appreciate the importance of rites of passage such as funerals, so they can talk to their children about them and let the children decide whether to attend or not.

CHAPTER 11

School Strategies for Renewal II

School staff have to respond to stress and loss in terms of the pastoral care of pupils when the occasion arises. However managing loss in schools has much wider implications. There are also curriculum responsibilities for the education of the pupil. If schools are to meet the overall requirements of the first section of Education Reform Act (1988) which states that children should be prepared for the responsibilities of adult life, then they need to consider issues of loss and stress. Bereavement and grief may be difficult aspects of the curriculum but they are part of life and schools not only have an important role in responding to loss, they have a crucial role in educating children about it. This chapter will consider different aspects of loss that school pupils may face.

Pastoral Support

The pastoral, social and emotion education (PSE) programme of a school by definition includes helping children develop sensitivity towards others and learning how people live and relate to each other. It covers religious and secular customs that regulate behaviour and pervades the whole ethos of the school. In any syllabus the issue of loss through divorce, death, disaster or whatever form needs to be addressed. In order to do this there is a vast collection of PSE material readily available from educational suppliers which will provide age-appropriate content. No matter how good the material is, it is severely restricted if the teacher or class tutor is not empathic; merely going through the motions is worse than useless. Active listening, good inter-personal skills and knowledge of group dynamics and group facilitation are all required.

Where a climate of trust and respect for children is established, the underlying values suffuse the whole life of the school. This means that when a child is bereaved for example, a parent will feel confident enough to inform the school staff and seek support for their child, if not for themselves. By staff here I mean all the staff from caretaker to headteacher, from secretaries to lunch time organisers. Children like adults talk to people they trust, not necessarily the person with the sign over the door saying 'Counsellor' or 'Head of Pastoral Care'.

Communication between home and school occasionally deteriorates following loss in the family. Letters home, or forms that need to be returned to school may not be dealt with because people are pre-occupied coping with the new life in which they find themselves. This does not indicate a drop in interest in the child's education, rather a temporary difficulty. Where there has been a divorce both parents may wish to be informed of the child's progress, so duplicate letters, reports and invitations will have to be sent. Discuss this with the parents and make sure that the child knows what arrangements have been made and why.

School staff should be informed on a need to know basis of arrangements made concerning a child's residence, details of contact orders and the like. Since the 1989 Children Act a person can apply for a contact order, and with the courts' permission so can the child. Knowledge about contact arrangements may prevent incidents in which a parent who has restricted contact comes to the school and causes an unpleasant encounter. Staff need to know of any legal injunctions and their implication for the school. If they are clear about the facts they can act with authority and confidence, take appropriate action and so avert stressful incidents.

Whilst courts make judgements about finance and access, children have the task of getting on with their lives and the reaction of the peer group is of paramount importance. As eleven-year-old David said, 'When my mum and dad split up. I wasn't that bothered, I was still a bit upset upset but what really got to me, what really didn't help was when people made fun of me about it.' Many youngsters, like David, repress feelings and suffer in silence. The teasing, the 'making fun' touches a raw nerve, it homes in on the way in which a child is different.

Some children feel they do not belong to 'real' families like other children in their class after a divorce or bereavement. As part of the PSE programme opportunities need to be taken in the classroom to assure children that people live in all sorts of family groupings. It will help dispel the myth of the model nuclear family. Children who are aware that these are unhelpful stereotypes are much less likely to take part in the kind of unpleasant teasing David experienced.

It is worth noting that siblings of children who have had serious illness may also develop a variety of problems similar to those seen in their returning sibling. If you bear this in mind and recognise it as part of the strain symptoms that the child has, you can find ways of managing it successfully. It should not be dismissed as attention seeking but treated with sensitivity.

Care of Teachers

Some children express grief more readily to a teacher or friend than within the family circle especially if there is a taboo about mentioning death at home. This means that teachers may find themselves listening to deep feelings of sorrow, hurt, anger and even despair. This is tiring, demanding work and its impact should not be underestimated. Teachers need to feel cared for and have someone from whom they can get support and compassion.

Teachers may be reluctant to discuss loss because of their own feelings, though they may explain this away by saying that the pupils would find it too difficult. This reaction is, to put it mildly, unhelpful. School staff need to consider what their own reactions to loss are in order to effectively help children in their care and staff training in handling loss should be part of ongoing professional development for staff.

Teachers are human – despite what some pupils think – when faced with a distressed child personal childhood experiences may be reawakened and cause pain. For example, a child returning to school after treatment for cancer may ignite fear about the disease and make it more difficult for the teacher to cope with the child's stress reactions of tiredness, irritability or anti-social behaviour. Also the teacher may be going through a similar life crisis which makes helping the pupil more difficult. Personal issues interfere in our relationships with others far more often than we think, so it is important to bear in mind our own 'unfinished business' and accept that when we have stressful events in our own lives it does effect our relationships, personal and professional.

Good staff peer support is essential in the healthy school. Strategies for renewal and growth apply to the staff as much as to the pupils, though I find this is all too often omitted when pastoral care programmes are designed. Who supports the staff is as important as who supports the children. Resources in the community such as specific self-help groups and community health networks can also provide support by giving talks to teachers about the nature of illness and loss and advise on ways the staff can help. This improves staff confidence. Also, teachers need to be encouraged to refer on those children who they feel they cannot help either because of personal issues in their own life, because their level of expertise is insufficient or because they feel 'stuck'. The decision to ask someone else to work with a child who has experienced loss, when you feel you are not meeting that child's needs, is a mark of professionalism not failure (Mallon 1987).

It is perfectly normal for teachers to be upset and to cry. If teachers can show feelings children get the message loud and clear that emotions are part of what makes us human and that grown-ups have them too. One teacher I worked with was very upset when a colleague died and she broke down in front of her tutor group. At the end of the period one boy came to her and for the first time since his father's suicide cried and asked her if he could talk to her. In floods of tears he explained that his mother was so angry with his father that she would not let anyone mention his name or, if he could not contain his distress, she got angry. With his teacher he was able at last to express his deep loss because she unwittingly gave him permission to grieve. Later, the teacher arranged counselling for the family and life is much improved for all of them now they are finally communicating again.

Death or Trauma During School Trips

Schools are particularly affected by the death of a pupil or staff member if this happens during a school trip or on school premises. The first shock tremors will carry all the characteristics described earlier in this book, and the interest of the media may impose extra strain; however there are a number of helpful strategies. If you are the form teacher and knew the pupil well, remember you will have your own feelings to deal with as well as those of the other pupils in your class. Whilst the child's name can easily be erased from the register, the feelings cannot be rubbed out. However tempting it may be, do not immediately shuffle the children round to different desks to 'close up' the space the dead child occupied. Leave the empty chair for a while, though not forever, and if possible let the class remove it or rearrange things when they are ready. If a new child is to join the class though, it is important they do not have to take that place as it may create difficulties. Try to resolve the seating before that point.

Give the children plenty of opportunity to talk about the dead person, what they liked and disliked so that they are not turned into an idealised saint. Remember they will have had enemies as well as best friends and everyone needs a chance to express their feelings and to share in the loss. The children may want to plan some kind of celebration of the pupils' life and display some of the latter's work.

One school in the north of England was affected by the death of a child whilst on a school trip. On the return to school, pupils found that a room had been set aside for children to use at any time. They did not have to seek permission but could decide for themselves. The headteacher was criticised by some of his staff who thought that other pupils would use the room as a way of avoiding lessons. That misuse never took place and pupils who used it saw it as a healing sanctuary.

Children need to know there is help at hand. Counsellors may be brought into school following a school trip or community disaster and children should have the option to see them. However this must be an option, not enforced counselling. Many pupils will find the support of their family, friends and teachers enough and not want specialised help. Strategies to handle loss of this dimension need to be discussed and in place prior to any incident taking place. Though the likelihood is small, discussions with staff and preparations in advance will greatly ease the strain should disaster strike. Any school which takes its responsibilities in this area seriously should develop a whole school approach to loss and actively plan what both their pastoral and emergency plans are, to address the needs of their pupils.

Educational Attainment After Loss

Unlike the long term affects of divorce, parental death appears to have little effect on later educational attainment. In a study by McClean and Wadsworth it was found that experience of death may actually increase a child's likelihood of going to university for those children whose families fell into the manual workers social group (McClean and Wadsworth 1988). In addition, in families where where a parent had died, parental re-marriage was significantly associated with an increased likelihood of higher educational attainment. However it is often the short term reactions to bereavement and its affect on academic performance which most concerns teachers.

When the child seems to be over the worst and initial reactions to bereavement have subsided there may be a period of disorganisation at school. The pupil may find it difficult to concentrate, seem aimless, not know how to set about tasks and have trouble finishing work. At this point it is useful to find practical support such as helping the child to build lists of words/pictures of things they need to do during the school day or before bedtime for example. This gives the child something tangible to hold on to and refer to during this disorganised phase. Plenty of time for play and social interaction should be made available also, as a way of moving through this phase.

Grieving takes up so much energy that there is often little left over for schoolwork, unless a pupil finds it a form of solace or escape. The preoccuptaion with their loss, whether the child is aware of it or not, may be frustrating for school staff who have concerns about attainments, National Curriculum targets and all the rest that go with the heavy demands of teaching, but the mourning child has his or her tasks too. The child needs time to recover. If you can accept that the emotional healing that the mourning process involves is crucial to the child's well-being as an adult, and that grieving is much better carried out immediately after the event rather than being postponed, then it may put attainment targets at school into perspective, patience is the key. The child can always retake a course. They can undertake the educational tasks later when they can concentrate *but* they may never regain full psychological well-being if they cannot grieve successfully, at their own pace, if they cannot mourn directly at the time they need to mourn.

If there are teachers in the school who have been trained in counselling and who have the time and facilities to run a regular group for children who have suffered loss, excellent supportive work can take place. Such groups need to be well organised and thought through, but in essence they offer a regular, structured time for the same small group to share in confidence their thoughts and feelings about what happened to them. It gives them an opportunity to work through their grief in a safe place with an adult skilled in responding to all their emotions but who is distant enough from the family to keep some sort of perspective. Given the shock to the family system following loss especially to the surviving parent, this type of intervention provides peer group support and education about grief, death and survival. It can facilitate the mourning process and so prevent a child getting stuck. Obviously, the children who form such a group should be offered the choice about attending and no one should be coerced.

One such group, described by Masterman and Reams report that the children who have taken part appear less constricted by their grief and less angry (Masterman and Reams 1986). They are much more able to cope with the emotional reactions they have had and are continuing to experience. The parents of these participants reported that there were decreased behaviour difficulties at home and at school and there was increased communication with their children about their bereavement which was previously avoided. Generally, both children and parents found the group a positive benefit.

Death on the curriculum

During 'Operation Desert Storm', as American troops fought in the Gulf in early 1992, schools in America found a place for death on the curriculum. Even before there were any casualties in the field, students were affected at home. As fathers, older brothers and sisters as well as members of the extended family were called away to fight – 300,000 children were at risk of losing a parent in the conflict because they were in the US Forces – teachers reported that many children were listless, irritable and unable to concentrate on their schoolwork. School counsellors, much more the norm in America than in England, were in constant demand, not just by pupils but by parents.

Linda Flies Carole, a psychotherapist with the National Childhood Grief Institute in Minneapolis, pointed out that the central issue for these young people was one of powerlessness. She stressed the need to try to keep everyday routines going. In some districts booklets were provided for teachers telling them how to respond to bereaved children and 'Quiet Rooms' were provided in which bad news could be broken or counselling provided. Military personnel visited classrooms to assure children that their parents in the forces were well trained and ready to handle combat.

Those involved in counselling emphasised the importance of helping children to focus on the things they could do to make life better or that were within their control. This was a way of reducing the pupils' feelings of powerlessness. Though many teachers fought against discussing the war in class, there was a great need for young people to discuss it, to try to make sense of it. It felt too important for them to ignore and in one case the result was unexpected. In Pittsburgh in January 1991, 150 students walked out of school as a protest against their schools' lack of attention to the war and their unwillingness to discuss their students' concerns about it.

During the Gulf War the National Union of Teachers issued a booklet entitled *The Gulf War: The Impact on Schools* in which it recommended strategies to alleviate stress children felt about the conflict. Those who had friends or relatives caught up displayed signs of disturbance including unusual tiredness. lack of concentration, and emotional instability. Children who are normally cheerful may be tearful, irritable, withdrawn or unusually involved in fights and quarrels because of the strain they are under. These typical stress reactions were detailed in the literature so teachers could acknowledge the reality of war for children.

Those children of different religious and ethnic minority groups had particular difficulties as they struggled to come to terms with the ambivalence inherent in the situation. It is easy to assume that children understand more than they do, so at the time it was important to reassure children that SCUD missiles could not reach Britain. The power of television news makes the images and proximity of the weapons too close for comfort. Getting the danger into perspective is one way of relieving the distress of children in times of war. Every child no matter what their religious or political inheritance, needs to feel secure and valued in school and any activities that can do this will be stress-reducing.

Bill Norris, in an article in the *Times Educational Supplement* (February 1991) brought the intertwined issues of war, violence and death into focus. He stated:

> The Gulf War has given dramatic focus to a problem which has been worrying US schools for some time. With gunfire in the city streets, an annual murder rate of 23,000, the advent of Aids and 5000 juvenile suicides a year, young people are touched by death everyday. Films and television abound with senseless violence. By the age of thirteen it is estimated that the average American child will have witnessed 10,000

cinematic deaths. By the age of eighteen one in twenty will have faced the death of a parent.

We cannot afford to ignore death in the school curriculum when faced with figures like these. On a very general level we can encourage children to express their grief and response to death both verbally and non-verbally through drawings, stories and play which will provide valuable outlets for feelings. As already pointed out, remember children can often sense when adults do not want to share their feelings and they mask them in order to please. Much better for the emotions to be out in the open than repressed and contaminating. Also, there is room to include historical, religious, cultural and social customs regarding death and dying right across the curriculum (Gatliffe 1988).

A Short Guide to Strategies for Schools

1. Ensure effective communication systems are in operation

Inform staff on a need to know basis whenever a child has experienced a major loss. This should be done as quickly as possible and in a sensitive way, putting a note in the register or on a staff notice board is not good enough.

2. Caring climate

Create a caring climate at school so that children can share their grief with classmates and so learn to accept that it is natural to show emotions – boys as well as girls. Watch out for any insensitive badgering of the child affected by loss.

3. Provide a 'Quiet Room'

It is very useful to have a 'Quiet Room', a bolt hole which can be used by children when they wish to be alone or have time out. Grieving children may suddenly feel a wave of sadness wash over them and they need a safe place where they can escape the glare of their peers.

4. Celebrate the life

Where a pupil has died the school can organise an assembly or some event which celebrates the life of the child as well as mourning his death. (This applies to staff as well.) Do acknowledge the death and talk to parents about what they would like the school to do.

5. Visit parents in their home where this is possible

Parents respond positively to teachers who take the time to visit and offer condolences. They may also need information about agencies that can help in the event of a child's death, for instance with funeral expenses. Parents may have other children at your school and may want to talk about their concerns for that child following the bereavement.

6. Counsellors need counselling

Find out where you can turn to for support. Bereavement causes much emotional turmoil and if you are working with children who have been affected by it then you will probably feel emotionally drained. Form a support network so that you can talk with others, this should help you and increase your effectiveness in dealing with your pupils and their families.

There is a section in Chapter Twelve on Materials and Resources which should be useful to any teachers concerned about helping children deal with loss.

CHAPTER 12

A Network of Support

In this final chapter there are some ideas about sources of help that you can turn to if you want assistance with a particular aspect of loss in childhood. As must have become quite obvious there is a great deal of common ground in terms of reactions or strategies to respond to the loss, whatever the cause. I have divided the areas so that you can more easily find specific areas of concern. I have included addresses, referral points, details of organisations, as well as books for both adults and children. There are bound to be omissions but remember your local Council for Voluntary Services, Citizens' Advice Bureaux and Social Services Department will have lists of relevant groups in your area. You should be able to consult resource directories in your local library, and of course your professional organisation should have suitable advice, training and resources to help.

Abuse
Support organisations

ChildLine
Royal Mail Building
Studd Street
London N1 0QW
Tel 0171 239 1000
Free helpline – 0800 1111

ChildLine could really go into any section listed here, since it is a service for children to use if they are worried about any problem whatsoever. It is a confidential telephone helpline, run by trained staff who will do whatever they can to enable the child to resolve their difficulties.

BASPCAN
British Association for the Study and Prevention of Abuse and Neglect
10 Priory Street
York
YO1 1EZ

For anyone working in the field who wants to know more about current research, legislation and training in this area. Provides a forum for discussion, information on research findings and professional support.

Kidscape Campaign for the Prevention of Sexual Assault on Children
152 Buckingham Palace Road
London SW1W 9TR
Tel: 0171 730 3300

Offers advice and educational guidance for anyone concerned about child abuse in whatever form. It has materials for children on how to avoid abuse, how to seek help and provides support for parents who may be concerned about their child. It also offers training courses for teachers and provides educational materials.

Keeping Deaf Children Safe
Willing House
356/364 Gray's Inn Road
London WC1X 8BH

Involved with the NSPCC in training and setting up programmes for deaf children to avoid abuse. They offer advice, support and materials for children with special educational needs.

The Anti-Bullying Campaign
10 Borough High Street
London SE1 9QQ

Set up by the parents of victims of bullying, ABC offers advice, support and counselling for parents and children. They also supply an information pack which includes strategies for use in school and guidance for teachers in combatting the problem.

NSPCC
67 Saffron Hill
London EC1N 8RS
0800 800 500

Anyone who is concerned about the welfare of a child can ring up their local NSPCC number for advice or to report their fears and these will be taken up by one of the trained members of staff. The NSPCC also runs training courses and will offer information and guidance related to child abuse. They also provide a booklet entitled *Protect Your Child; A Guide about Child Abuse for Parents* which is available free of charge.

Books for adults

Morris, M. (1998) *If I Should Die Before I Wake.* London: Souvenir Press.
Deals with sexual abuse and incest.

Spring, J. (1987) *Cry Hard and Swim: The Story of an Incest Survivor.* London: Virago.
The true story of the childhood and therapy of an incest survivor – the author herself. Whilst recounting the abuse that happened within a family which appeared reasonably well-off both emotionally and materially, it moves on to the show the healing process that she the child/adult underwent.

Books for children

Elliot, M. (1986) *The Willow Street Kids: 'It's Your Right To Be Safe'.* London: Marlyn Books.
This fictionalised account for older primary school children of actual events of attempted abuse as told by two girls, includes the approach of 'The Stranger' and how to deal with the 'bad secret' of unwanted attentions from an uncle. Good fiction and healthy, empowering messages for children.

Howard, E. (1987) *Gillyflower.* London: Collins.
A moving story about a twelve year old girl's experience of sexual abuse by her father. She realises that she has to take action that might damage the family in order to repair her life. It shows the complexities of the situation and just how trapped someone in Gilly's position can be.

Magorian, M. (1983) *Goodnight, Mr Tom.* London: Penguin.
As an evacuee from London Will discovers warmth and love in the care of Mr Tom. This brilliant book encorporates many aspects of loss from physical abuse, rejection by his mother and death, yet remains a story full of hope and trust regained.

National Children's Home (1986) *It's O.K. to say No.* London: Peter Haddock Ltd.

Bereavement
Support organisations

The Alder Centre
Royal Liverpool Children's Hospital,
Alder Hey
Liverpool L12 2AP

Offers support to all those affected by the death of a child. Volunteers, who have themselves been affected by such loss and trained counsellors provide help for adults and children. There is a telephone helpline available too.

The Compassionate Friends
6 Denmark Street
Bristol BS1 5DQ

A self-help group for parents who have lost a son or daughter. They have two sub-groups for parents of murdered children and one for parents of suicide victims. They also have a library from which you may borrow books and tapes.

CRUSE Bereavement Care
Cruse House
126 Sheen Road
Richmond
Surrey TW9 1UR

Bereavement care provided by trained counsellors, plus advice and information on practical problems and befriending.

Gay Bereavement Project
Unitarian Rooms
Hoop Lane
London NW11 8BS
Tel. 0181 455 8894

Provides advice and support.

Institute of Family Therapy
43 New Cavendish Street
London W1M 7RG

The Institute's Elizabeth Raven Memorial Fund offers free counselling to recently bereaved families or those with seriously ill family members. They work with the whole family.

The Foundation For The Study of Infant Deaths
5th Floor
4 Grosvenor Place
London SW1

Anyone affected by sudden infant deaths, 'cot death', will find advice, support and information provided. Local Citizen's Advice Bureaux give information and advice on matters related to death including funeral arrangements and disposal of possessions.

Books for adults

Downey, A. (1990) *Dear Stephen*. London: Arthur James.

A moving book written after her bright, outwardly successful son took his own life. It reveals the conflicting emotions and thoughts surrounding those bereaved by suicide.

Fabian, A. (1988) *The Daniel Diary*. London: Grafton Books.

Five year old Sarah Fabian died suddenly after she had contracted a 'flu virus. Her younger brother, three-year-old Daniel, was devastated by this and his mother recorded his painful, valiant attempts to come to terms with her loss. The book shows how young children mourn and it may help others with very young children faced with their own loss. About bereavement but also the courage and inventiveness of childhood.

Jones, M. (1988) *Secret Flowers*. London: Women's Press.

This book is written by a woman whose husband died suddenly of cancer. She speaks of the desolation, disbelief, rage and loss as well as the astonishing moments of joy she felt.

Pennells, Sister M. and Smith, S. S. (1995) *The Forgotten Mourners: Guidelines for Working with Bereaved Children*. London: Jessica Kingsley Publishers.

A practical guide with lots of helpful ideas and sensitive insight.

Tittensor, J. (1984) *Year One: A Record*. Harmondsworth: Penguin.

The author lost his son aged nine and daughter aged seven in a fire at the house of his estranged wife. The book chronicles his life after this tragedy.

Wells, R. (1988) *Helping Children Cope With Grief*. London: Sheldon Press.

Rosemary's husband died when her children were seventeen, fourteen and eleven years old. Her practical insights based on personal experiences reflect the reality of living with children coming to terms with the death of someone they love.

What To Do After A Death DSS leaflet D49.

The raw facts about practical matters that have to be dealt with when someone dies.

Wilkinson, T. (1991) *The Death Of A Child, A Book For Families*. London: Julia MacRae Books.

Tessa was a bereavement counsellor for the Helen House Children's Hospice in Oxford. Her book is for adults and children to read. Gentle and empathic, the book is divided into different sections so that parts can be read by the child on his own, parents and other parts which are meant to be read together. A sensitive, caring book which provides much comfort and reassurance.

Books for children

Burns, P. (1987) *The Far Side Of Shadow.* London: Harvestime Publications.
Story of bereavement and after as it affects a child.

Nystrom, C. (1988) *Emma Says Goodbye.* An Albatross Book, Lion Publishing.

Simmonds, P. (1989) *Fred.* London: Puffin.
A wonderfully told tale of the death of a cat and his amazing funeral with characteristically quirky illustrations.

Divorce and Separation

Support organisations

Mediation and Conciliation Services
The National Family Conciliation Council
Shaftesbury Avenue
Percy Street
Swindon SN2 2AZ

National Council for One Parent Families
255 Kentish Town Road
London NW5 2LX

Seeks to improve conditions for one parent families and offers advice to families in need of help.

Relate: National Marriage Guidance
Herbert Gray College
Little Church Street
Rugby CV21 3AP
Tel: 01788 573241

Offers support, information and counselling to those who are having relationship difficulties including unmarried couples, gay and lesbian couples.

Stepfamily
The National Step-Family Association
162 Tennison Road
Cambridge CB1 2DP

Offers practical help, support and information to all members of stepfamilies.

Books for adults

Blume, J. (1987) *Letters To Judy: What Kids Wish They Could Tell You*. London: Pan.

Garlick, H. (1989) *The Separation Survival Handbook*. London: Penguin.

Books for children

Blume, J. (1979) *It's Not The End Of The World*. London: Heinemann.

> Eleven-year-old Grainne said, 'I once dreamt that I was Karen in Judy Blume's *It's Not The End Of The World*. This confused me but prepared me too. Karen's parents were splitting up and it shows what troubles they went through.'

Brown, L. K. and Brown, M. (1987) *Dinosaurs Divorce: A Guide For Changing Families*. London: Collins.

> The authors, themselves both divorced, present different aspects of divorce as seen through a child's eyes. Aimed at children under ten, it has delightful pictures accompanying a sensitive text that faces the uncomfortable emotions raised by divorce including fear and anger. It's a good book for parents and children to read together since it provides an easy way to talk about divorce through the events that happen in dinosaur land.

Burns, P. (1991) *Nothing Ever Stays The Same*. Lion Publishing.

> Sandie's parents are split up. Her mother does not seem to like her anymore and she can't stay with her father either. So what can she do? Aimed at twelve-year-olds.

Fine, A. (1989) *Goggle Eyes*. Harmondsworth: Hamish Hamilton.

> Kitty is coming to terms with changes in her Mum and her new suitor. With an ingenious ending and lots of energy, it tackles relevant issues in a very readable way. Great fun. Nine years plus.

Hughes, S. (1987) *Alfie Lends A Hand*. London: Bodley Head.

> Alfie lives with his baby sister and his Mum. Very well illustrated, it tells of the time Alfie goes to his first birthday party and takes his old blanket 'comforter' with him to help him get over his fear. A firm favourite with my children between three and six years old.

Nystrom, C. (1991) *Mike's Lonely Summer*. Oxford: Lion Publishing.

> This child's guide to divorce is sensible and down to earth. Like others in this series by the same author, each book combines a story with boxes of information, question and comment

The National Council for One Parent Families has a guide to books for children and young adults living in one parent families. Called *We Don't All Live With Mum and Dad* it provides a whole range of useful titles.

Illness

Support organisations

ACT

Association for Children with Life Threatening Conditions and Their Families
Institute of Child Health
Royal Hospital for Sick Children
St. Michael's Hill
Bristol BS2 8BJ

National Resource and Information Service available to help with all aspects of illness in childhood.

BACUP

121/123 Charterhouse Street
London EC1M 6AA
Tel 0800 181 199

Helps patients, their families and friends cope with cancer. Trained cancer nurses provide information, emotional support and practical advice by telephone or letter.

Cancer Research Campaign

Wilmslow Road
Withington
Manchester M20

An information booklet *Welcome Back*, is available for teachers of children returning to school after treatment for cancer. It has been written to help teachers understand more about childhood cancer, its treatment and the problems it can cause children at school. It gives practical advice on how to help the child and his siblings cope. The booklet is available free to teachers through the relevant pediatric oncology treatment centre the child has attended.

Eating Disorders Association

Sackville Street
44 Magdalen Street
Norwich NR3 1JU
Tel 01603 664915
Helpline 01603 621414

National Association for the Welfare of Children in Hospital
Argyle House
29–31 Euston Road
London NW1 2SD
Advice on any matter relating to children in hospital.

MAC Helpline
The Cancer Relief Macmillan Fund
15/19 Britten Street
London SW3 3TZ
0800 591026

This free telephone helpline is for teenagers with cancer or who have had cancer, their family and friends, indeed anyone involved who wants to talk to a friendly, specially trained, counsellor who can also give information about self-help groups. They operate a networking service supplying the names of other teenage cancer patients in the caller's area.

The Malcolm Sargent Cancer Fund for Children
14 Abingdon Road
London W8 6AF

Can provide cash grants for parents of children (up to the age of 21) with cancer to help pay for clothing, equipment, travel etc. Applications through a hospital social worker who will fill in a form on the patient's behalf. Available anywhere in the UK.

The Sick Children's Trust
10 Guilford Street
London WC1N 1DT

Local hospitals have in some cases bereavement counsellors or others who can assist when professional help is needed following a bereavement. Your GP, Social Services Department or Well Women Clinic should have information.

St Christopher's Hospice
51–59 Lawrie Park Road
London SE22 6DZ

Publications, training and general information about hospice work and bereavement.

Books for adults
Lewis, D. (1989) *Helping Your Anxious Child*. London: Methuen.

Books for children

Bales, H. (1987) *What's Up Mate?* London: Hodder & Stoughton.

A book specially written for children between five and twelve, who have been recently diagnosed with cancer or leukemia so they can learn about their illness and its treatment.

Bergman, T. (1989) *One Day At A Time: Children Living With Leukemia.* London: Gareth Steven's Children's Books.

Actual photographs of children in hospital which follows their stories. It includes questions from children, such as 'What is cancer?', What is the treatment for leukemia?' and gives simple straightforward answers which do not patronise children.

Gillespie, J. (1989) *Brave Heart: The Diary of a Nine-Year-Old Girl Who Refused to Die.* London: Century.

Joanne's delightful illustrations accompany her text. 'I decided to write this book,' she says, 'because when I was frightened and not sure of myself in hospital there was nothing for me to read. There were books for grown-ups but there were none for children. So I decided to write this book for other children who are like me feeling frightened and ill. And I hope it will help them to feel a bit more sure of themselves.'

Nystrom, C. (1990) *Emma Says Goodbye.* Oxford: Lion Publishing Series.

Aunty Sue is young, strong and lively. Emma finds her way of coming to terms with Sue's illness and death. Age 12+.

Reuter, E. (1989) *Christopher's Story.* London: Hutchison.

A beautifully illustrated story about a boy with leukemia. Gentle and sensitive story for junior age range children.

Mental Health
Support organisations

MIND
National Association for Mental Health
Granta House
15 –19 Broadway
Stratford
London E15 4BQ
0181 519 2122

For anyone seeking advice/support regarding mental health difficulties.

Mental Health Foundation
37 Mortimer Street
London W1N 8JU
0171 580 0145

Young Minds
102 –108 Clerkenwell Road
London EC1M 5SA
0171 336 8445

Mental health issues for children and young people and anyone who needs advice to help them.

Eating Disorders Association
Sackville Place
44 Magdalen Street
Norwich,
Norfolk NR3 1JE

Al-Anon & Al-ateen Al-Anon Family Groups
61 Great Dover Street
London SE1 4YF

Al-Ateen is for the teenage children of problem drinkers, offering advice and counselling as well as general information.

More General Resources

Organisations

National Children's Bureau
8 Wakley Street
London EC1V 7QE

As well as conducting research into all aspects of children's lives the bureau publishes a magazine called *Who Cares?*. It comes out every three months and is written for, and partly by, young people in care.

National Association for Children of Alcoholics
PO Box 64
Fishponds
Bristol BS16 2UH
0800 289061

Offers advice, information and fellowship to children of alcoholics as well as running conferences and training for those involved with children of alcoholics.

National Association for the Welfare of Children in Hospital
Argyll House
29–31 Euston Road
London NW1 2SD
Tel 0171–833–2041

NORCAP
3 New High Street
Headlington
Oxford OX3 7AJ

An organisation to help anyone involved in adoption be they children tracing natural parents, parents tracing children, or siblings of adopted children. It offers advice, counselling and support to trace relatives.

British Association for Counselling
1 Regent Place
Rugby
Warwickshire CV21 2PJ
Tel: 01788 578328

Concerned with all varieties of counselling, the information office publishes directories listing counselling services and will refer enquirers to an experienced local counsellor.

The Samaritans Youth Outreach
17 Uxbridge Road
Slough SL1 1SN

After conducting the funeral service of a fourteen year old girl who committed suicide because when her periods started, she did not know what was happening and thought she must have VD, Chad Varah set up the Samaritans in 1953. Befriending, counselling and outreach work with young people are all part of their nationwide work still very much in demand – and expanding – forty years later. Offers help with any sort of problem.

Children with Special Needs

Organisations

Royal National Institute for the Blind
224 Great Portland Street
London W1N 6AA

The National Library for the Handicapped Child
20 Bedford Way
London WC1L 0AL

This offers materials for the 'print handicapped child'. Those who have visual impairment or are physically disabled so that they cannot handle books adequately, or turn pages for instance. Activities, books and advice as well as plenty of books that show disabled people as the central characters.

The National Autistic Society
393 City Road
London EC1V 1NE
Tel: 833 2299

The Dyslexia Institute
133 Gresham Road
Staines
Middlesex TW18 2AJ

Advice and guidance on diagnosis and educational support for dyslexic children.

ERIC Eneuresis Resource and Information Centre Bedwetting advice
65 St. Michael's Hill
Bristol BS2 8DZ.

They provide advice and up to date information on treatment and newsletter with practical advice and tips, as well as *Eric's Wet To Dry Bedtime Book* for children aged 7–14 years.

Organisations offering support to children

This part is longer than the others in this chapter simply because teacher may need a wider overview of the whole issue of loss if they are to introduce it into their schools.

Materials for use in schools

The subject of loss general can be successfully introduced into a variety of areas in schools, dramatherapy, hospitals, counselling or in any therapeutic setting concerned with the well-being of children. It is always important to check out with the person – teacher, key worker, etc. – who has primary care of the child, to find out if there is any recent event which might make the subject material too stressful for him or her to handle. If a child has just been bereaved for instance, it might be more appropriate to defer using the material if it deals with loss. Children should be encouraged to take part in discussions, by asking questions and being actively involved, but no child should be forced to talk. Sensitivity is the keynote. No one should be pressured into talking about their feelings or experiences. When children feel sufficiently safe and emotionally able to participate verbally they will do so, but they can still gain a great deal by listening to others, including a caring teacher. Literature offers an endless source of material on bereavement, separation and loss which can be read aloud to whole groups or available to individuals for personal reading. Additionally the writing of children themselves can provide an excellent jumping off point for all kinds of creative therapeutic work which may be extended in ways which are appropriate to their developmental level, or used purely as a stimulus for discussion and groupwork. You may find the following useful, taken from The Cadbury's 8th Book for Children's Poetry: Prize winning poetry from children throughout Great Britain:

My Grandad

Grandad Lea
Was getting old.
He's gone to Baby Jesus
To help him do his stuff.

Matthew Lea (4)

My Granny

My Granny died.
They let her body
Stay in the house.
My Mammy went to see her
And she brought me.
When she seen my Granny
She started to cry.
But me, Just sitting
On a seat, reading my book
Not crying at all.

Dominic Malarnon (7)

Father

Father is kind and friendly but sometimes mean.
Your love is strong and tight all through the night
But soon he, and other people his age and older,
Will leave us and enter the World of Wonders and Dreams
Alone.

Ty Murray (8)

Dad

Dad was someone who had everything
In the right place –
Including his heart.
He never called us little terrors.
He always called us the little ones or the kids.
He never hit us, but told us reasons why
(when we weren't reasonable).
He wore smart shoes, comfortable trousers.
When you tried his shoes on
they were warm.
But when the time came for him to leave us
there was no warm feeling in his shoes.
No warmth or familiar smell in the clothing –
Nothing.
And he left a gap in the word comfort able.

Julia Wearn (11)

When I Am Lonely

When I am lonely
and my brother will not play with me,
I feel like the last petal
left on a flower
and the other petals
are floating away.

Victoria Evans (6)

My Mum's Father

In Finland,
Before I was born,
My Mum's father,
Hid most of his weapons,
In the cellar,
At the bottom of the house.
Some people
Found out.

He was taken prisoner,
And a few weeks later
He was set free again,
And he died a few years after.
My Grandmother has a picture
Of my Grandad
And I cry
Every time
I look at it.

Lucy Golding (7)

Stories

Stories can provide a useful way of introducing discussions about death, particularly with younger children. They can be used to help bereaved children or those who have lost contact with a parent through divorce or imprisonment for example. By facing troublesome issues at one remove, through the medium of the story, they have an opportunity to explore. You can make up your own stories. This one I devised to help children face the issue of guilt following the death of a parent.

BRACKEN'S BURDEN

Once upon a time, in a wood, there lived a young red squirrel called Bracken. The wood was sometimes bright and sunny and sometimes cool and a bit scary. Bracken lived alone with his mother because his father had died.

Bracken had a lot of mixed feelings about his Dad's death. One feeling he found hardest, the one he told nobody about, was that maybe, he had made his Dad die. You see, the day before his Dad died, Bracken did something wrong and his Dad had shouted at him. Bracken felt very cross and wished his Dad would go away and leave him alone. Then, the very next day, his Dad was dead! Bracken thought 'If I had been a good squirrel maybe my Dad wouldn't have died.'

When he sat by himself on the low tree branch, Bracken felt awful about this. He loved his Dad and wished he were alive again. Bracken was sitting there sadly thinking about how it might be his fault when his mother came up to him. She sat very close to him and stroking his soft fur she said, 'I miss Daddy too, you know. It feels bad that he died, doesn't it?'

'Yes,' Bracken replied, 'But if I'm a really good squirrel can he come back alive again?'

'No,' Mother Squirrel answered. 'We would both like Daddy to be alive again but that can never happen. There is nothing we can do to make him alive again.'

Bracken looked down and whispered, 'I wish I had been good. If had been good then Daddy would not have died.'

'What do you mean?' mother asked.

'Daddy shouted at me the day before he died. I was naughty then he died and I caused it.' Bracken really believed it was his fault.

Mother said, 'No, Bracken you did not make Daddy die. Even if you had been good the day before, your Daddy would still have died. You did not kill him.'

'But Daddy shouted at me to be good and I wished he would go away, and now he's gone forever.'

Mother Squirrel spoke to her young one gently, 'That's not how it happens. A young one cannot make a parent die by being bad or feeling angry. Your Daddy died because he got sick. Your Daddy died because of the sickness and because we don't have any forest remedies to fight that illness. You did not kill him.'

Bracken looked up. He felt just the tiniest bit better. 'I suppose you're right Mum. I didn't make Daddy die but I still wish he was alive.'

'Me too,' said Mother Squirrel hugging him close, 'We both wish he was still alive and with us, but he is dead and there is nothing we can do to bring him back and it isn't our fault that he died.'

Bracken's mother was right. Children do not make their parents die. Sometimes they think it is their fault for being naughty or doing something bad and that if they had been good nothing would have happened. But that it not true. It was not Bracken's fault.

FOLLOW UP

After a story like this the teacher can ask pupils what they thought about Bracken's ideas. The children might draw parallels with their own lives. Usually, only some of the children can talk openly about personal experiences which could be connected to this story, however even the ones who listen will gain insight. Respect for their choice is of paramount importance. Another way to follow up this story would be to ask the children to write a letter to Bracken. The aim of the letter might be to comfort him. Or, the children might write a letter to Mother Squirrel giving her more ideas about how she might help her son feel better. This exercise is useful in focusing childrens attention on helpful ways of responding to bereavement.

Organisations

All the organisations already mentioned will have literature and information which will be helpful to you in school. There are more, of course, but here are a few additional ones because they address the problems of children's stress/loss which may directly impinge on school life.

National Eczema Society
Tavistock House
East Tavistock Square
London WC1H 9SR

As many children suffer from eczema at times of stress, and as others with severe eczema may have special needs at school, this society have provided guidelines to assist. It is called *A Practical Guide To The Management of Eczema in Schools*, which includes tips for parents and school staff and is available from the above address.

National Children's Bureau Library and Information Service
8 Wakley Street
London EC1V 7QE

Open to everyone working with or interested in the field of children and their care. Unique information service.

The Samaritans (Address above)

In 1993 the Samaritans launched a resource pack for teachers as part of their campaign to focus on the stresses facing young people today. It includes material for topic work, drama and role play as well as creative writing and poetry. It can be used in National Curriculum areas of study including English, personal, social and moral education as well as RE and Home Economics, since it relates to homes and families as well as the wider community.

Trust for the Study of Adolescence
Tel: 01273 693311

Carries out research into issues affecting adolescents and has packs covering Suicide and Self-harm; Family Breakdown.

Books for children

BBC Books (1989) *Children At War.* London: BBC Books.
   Twelve survivors look back at their wartime childhoods in far-flung parts of the world.

Coppard, Y. (1990) *Bully.* Oxford: Bodley Head.

The hero Kerry, crippled after an accident dramatically tackles the boy who teases and bullies her. His secret gives her the key!

Dahl, R. (1986) *Boy*. London: Penguin.

This first part of Roald Dahl's autobiography includes all manner of loss: when he was three his sister died from appendicitis, a few months later his father died and his mother, seven months pregnant when her husband died, had to cope alone in the foreign land that was England. Dahl's touch is captivating and powerfully evokes the feelings of loss yet sustains hope for the future.

Dixon, P. (1991) *AIDs and you*. Kingsway Publications.

Mainly aimed at young children who know someone with AIDS.

Doherty, B. (1989) *Spellhorn*. London: Lions.

This exciting adventure story arose from the author's work with four blind children. The heroine, Laura is blind but sees with her mind's eye and senses the existence of a special world of her own in which the last unicorn, Spellhorn, plays a crucial part.

Frank, A. (1954) *The Diary of Ann Frank*. London: Pan Books.

Ann Frank wrote her diary in hiding from Nazi terror in an Amsterdam attic from 1942 to 1944, when she was aged between 13 and 15. As a beacon of hope in the darkest times it portrays adolescent hopes and fears in the face of great loss.

Hessell, J. (1989) *Nobody's Perfect*. London: Hutchison.

This is the story of a child who dies. At school his friends react in many ways to his death and the book shows how death can effects friends as well as family. A useful book to have in schools to act as the basis for discussion unrelated to a school event of this nature.

Holm, A. (1979) *I Am David*. London: Methuen.

Prize winning fiction for older readers, this book is about a boy who escapes from a camp during World War II and tramps his way across Europe searching for his identity and a family. Full of hope and tenderness.

McEwan, I. (1985) *Rose Blanche*. London: Jonathan Cape.

Delightful illustrations intensify the tragedy of this story in which Rose, seeing the changes in her small German village, gradually becomes aware of what is happening to the people the army takes away. The dawning of the horrifying truth brings home the message of how innocence is destroyed by the brutality of war. Beautifully written.

Sanders, P. (199) *Let's Talk About Death And Dying.* Gloucester Press: Aladdin Books.

> Part of a series for use in schools. These books tackle sensitive issues including divorce, abortion and illness. This book aimed at junior school children has lots of pictures and a simple, easily understood text.

Ward, B. (1989) *Good Grief.* London: Jessica Kingsley Publishers.

> This is an education 'pack' containing background information to the subject of bereavement and its effect on children, and it provides age relevant exercises for use in schools. Age range – up to eleven years.

BIBLIOGRAPHY

Andersonn, E. (1988) 'Siblings of mentally handicapped children and their social relations.' *British Jnl. Special Education 15*, 1, Research Supplement, 24–26.

Anthony, E.J. and Benedek, T. (1975) *Depression and Human Existence.* Boston: Little, Brown.

Ayalon, O. and Flasher, A. (1993) *A. Chain Reaction: Children and Divorce.* London: Jessica Kingsley Publishers Ltd.

Best, P. (1984) 'An experience on interpreting death to children.' *Pastoral Care 1*, 2.

Bettleheim, B. (1987) *A Good Enough Parent.* London: Thames and Hudson.

Black, D. and Unbanowicz, M.A. (1987) 'Family intervention with bereaved children.' *Journal of Child Psychology and Psychiatry 28*, 3.

Bowlby, J. (1960) 'Grief and mourning in infancy and early childhood.' *Psychoanalytic Study of the Child 15*, 9.

Bowlby, J. (1970) *(Attachment) Attachment and Loss Vol 1.* London: Hogarth Press.

Bowlby, J. (1973) *(Separation, Anxiety and Anger) Attachment and Loss, Vol. 2.* London: Hogarth Press.

Bowlby J. (1980) *Loss, Sadness and Depression,* Volume III of Attachment and Loss Series, London: Hogarth Press.

Bowlby, J. (1980) *Attachment and Loss* Vol. III. London: Hogarth Press.

Bowlby, J. (1988) *A Secure Base.* London: Routledge.

Bowlby, J. (1991) *Charles Dickens: A Biography.* London: Hutchison.

Burgess, A.W., Hartman, C.R. and Kelley, S.J. (1990) 'Assessing child abuse: the triad checklist.' *Journal of Psychosocial Nursing 28*, 4.

Cartwright, R.D. *et al.* (1984) 'Broken dreams: a study of the effects of divorce and depression on dream content.' *Psychiatry USA.*

Cleary, J. (1986) 'Parental involvement in the lives of children in hospital.' *Archives of Disease In Childhood 61.*

Cline, F.W. and Rothenberg, M.B. (1974) 'Preparation of a child for major surgery: a case report.' *Journal of the American Academy of Child Psychiatry 13*, 78–94.

Cohen, F. (1978) 'Art therapy after accidental death of a sibling.' In C.E. Shaefer and H.L. Millman (eds) *Therapies For Children.* New York: Josey-Bass.

Conrad, N. (1991) 'Where do they turn? Social support systems of suicidal High School Adolescents.' *Journal Psychosocial Medicine 29*, 3.

Coote, A., Harman, H. and Hewitt, P. (1991) *Family Way: A New Approach to Policy Making.* London: The Institute of Public Policy Research.

Craft, M. and Craft, A. (1978) *Sex and The Mentally Handicapped.* London: Routledge and Kegan Paul.

Dahl, R. (1986) *Boy.* London: Penguin.

Davids, A. (1974) *Children in Conflict.* New York: Wiley.

Elliot, M. (1985) *Preventing Child Sexual Assault.* London: Bedford Square Press.

Erikson, E. (1965) *Childhood and Society.* Harmondsworth: Penguin.

Fahrenback, P., Smith, T., Monasteresky, M. and Deshar, A., Smith, R. (1986) 'Adolescent sexual offenders, offenders and offense characteristics.' *American Journal of Orthopsychiatry 56,* 2, April.

Flach, F.F. and Draghi, S.C. (eds) (1975) *The Nature and Treatment of Depression.* New York: Wiley.

Freud, S. (1957) *Mourning and Melancholia.* Standard Edition. *14,* 243. London: Hogarth Press.

Freud, A. (1981) *Child Sexual Abuse Within The Family.* London: CIBA Foundation, Tavistock Publications Ltd.

Garlick, H. (1990) 'Easing the pain for children after divorce.' *Guardian,* Oct. 31.

Gatliffe, E.D. (1988) *Death In The Classroom: A Resource Book for Teachers and Others.* London: Epworth Press.

Gleser, G., Green, B. and Winget, C. (1981) *Prolonged Psychosocial Effects Of Disaster: A Study of Buffalo Creek.* Academic Press USA.

Gordon, L. (1989) *Heroes Of Their Own Lives: A Study of 120 Years of Sexual Abuse in America.* London: Virago.

Grollman, E.A. (ed) (1967) *Explaining Death To Children.* Boston: Beacon Press.

Halsey, N. and Dennis, N. (1991) Research carried out by the Institute for Economic Affairs.

Hawton, K. (1986) *Suicide and Attempted Suicide Among Children.* London: Sage.

Hersey, J. (1972) *Hiroshima: The Experiences of Six Survivors.* London: Penguin.

Hughes, J. A. (1995) *Understanding Classical Sociology.* London: Sage Publications.

Jewett, C. (1984) *Helping Children Cope With Separation and Loss.* London: Batsford Academic Press.

Judd, D. (1990) *Give Sorrow Words: Working With A Dying Child.* London: Free Association Books.

Kempe, C.H. and Helfer, R.E. (1972) *Helping the Battered Child and his Family.* Oxford: Lippincott.

Kerfoot, M. (1988) 'Deliberate self-poisoning in childhood and early adolescence.' *Journal of Child Psychology and Psychiatry 29,* 3.

Kiernan, K. (1991) 'National Child Development Study of 17,000 children.' *Family Policy Studies Centre Bulletin.* Winter.

Koocher, G.P. (1974) 'Conversations with children about death.' *Journal of Clinical Child Psychology 13,* 2.

Kroth, J.A. (1978) 'Family Therapy impact on intrafamilial child sexual abuse.' Presented at the Second International Congress of Child Abuse and Neglect, London: September.

Kübler-Ross, E. (1970) *On Death And Dying.* London: Tavistock.

Kübler-Ross, E. (1978) *To Live Until We Say Goodbye.* Boston: Prentice-Hall USA.

Kübler-Ross, E. (1980) *Death and Dying.* London: Tavistock Press.

Kübler-Ross, E. (1983) *On Children And Death.* London: Macmillan.

Lawrence, M. (1984) *The Anorexic Experience.* London: The Women's Press Handbook Series.

Lifton, R. J. (1967) *Death in Life: The Survivors of Hiroshima.* London: Wedenfeld and Nicholson.

Lindemann, E. (1979) *Beyond Grief.* New York: Jason Aronson.

Lonsdale, G. *et al.* (1979) *Children, Grief and Social Work.* Oxford: Oxford University Press.

Macaskill, A. and Monarch, J.H. (1990) 'Coping with childhood cancer: the case for long term counselling help for parents.' *British Journal of Guidance and Counselling 18*, 1.

MacClean, M. and Wadsworth, M.E. (1988) 'The interests of children after parental divorce: a long term perspective.' *International Journal of Law and the Family 2*.

Mahler, M.S. (1950) 'Helping children to accept death.' *Child Study 27*.

Maisch, H. (1973) *Incest.* New York: Stein and Day.

Mallon, B. (1987) *Counselling Children With Special Educational Needs.* Manchester University Press.

Mallon, B. (1987) *An Introduction To Counselling For Special Educational Needs.* Manchester: Manchester University Press.

Mallon, B. (1989) *Children Dreaming.* London: Penguin.

Mallon, B. (1989) *An Introduction To Counselling Skills For Special Educational Needs.* Manchester: Manchester University Press.

Martin, P. (1997) *The Sickening Mind.* London: Harper-Collins.

Masterman, S.H. and Reams, R. (1986) 'Support groups for bereaved preschool and school age children.' *American Journal of Orthopsychiatry 58*, 4, October.

Medler, B.W. (1985) 'Identification and treatment of stepfamily issues for counsellors and teachers.' Paper presented at the Annual Convention of the American Association of Counselling and Development, New York, April.

Miller, A. (1987) *For Your Own Good, The Roots of Violence in Child-Rearing.* London: Virago.

Miller, A. (1991) *Breaking Down The Wall of Silence.* London: Virago.

Miller, A. (1991) 'Honour They Father and Mother: No Way.' *The Guardian,* September 15.

Mitchell, A. (1985) *Children in the Middle.* London: Tavistock.

Monroe, M. (1975) *My Story.* London: W. H. Allen.

National Children's Bureau (1980) *A Fairer Future for Children: Towards Better Parental and Professional Care.* London: NCB.

Norris, B. (1991) Article in *Times Educational Supplement,* February.

Nuffield CPU (1995) Research from Nuffield Child Psychiatric Unit, University of Newcastle.

Oaklander, V. (1975) *Windows To Our Children: A Gestalt Therapy Approach to Children and Adolescents.* Moab, UT: Real People Press.

O'Day, B. (1983) *Preventing Sexual Abuse in Persons with Disabilities.* Santa Cruz: Network Publications.

Parker, S.D. RN, MSN (1988) 'Accident or suicide? Do life change events lead to adolescent suicide?' *Journal of Psychosocial Nursing 26,* 6.

Pettle, M.S.A. and Lansdown, R.G. (1986) 'Adjustment to death of a sibling.' *Archives of Disease of Childhood 61,* 278–283.

Poznanski, G. and Krull, J.P. (1970) 'Childhood depression.' *Archives of General Psychiatry 23,* 4.

Rosenblatt, R. (1983) *Children of War.* New York: Anchor Press.

Rush, F. (1980) *The Best Kept Secret.* Boston: McGraw-Hill.

Rutter, M. (1966) *Children of Sick Parents.* London: OUP.

Ryerson, E. (1984) *Sexual Abuse and Self-Protection Education For Developmentally Delayed Youth; A Priority Need.* Sex Education Council for the United States, New York, SIECUS Report 1984; 13; 1; 6–7.

Samson, D. (1988) *Children in Hospitals: An evaluation of a pre-admission preparation package.* Unpublished MSc dissertation, Birmingham University.

Siegel, K., Mesagno, F.P. and Grace, Christ M.S.W. (1990) 'A prevention program for bereaved children.' *American Journal of Orthopsychiatry 60,* 2, April.

Smith, S.C. and Pennells, M. (1995) *Interventions With Bereaved Children.* London: Jessica Kingsley.

Spinetta, J.J. (1974) 'The dying child's awareness of death: a review.' *Psychological Bulletin 81.*

Stubbs, D. (1992) Samaritans outreach worker in 'The Big One', *Young Guardian* March 31.

Sunday Times (1986) 'Dear Esther...' 9 November.

Tatelbaum, J. (1981) *The Courage To Grieve.* London: Heinemann.

Terr, L.C. (1987) 'Nightmares in children.' In C. Guilleminault (ed) *Sleep and Its Disorders In Children.* New York: Raven Press.

Tysoe, M. (1986) 'The Hurt That Won't Go Away'. *Guardian,* August 12.

UNICEF (1991) *The State of the World's Children.* London: UNICEF.

Varma, V. (1993) *How and Why Children Fail.* London: Jessica Kingsley.

Wallerstein, J. and Kelly, J.B. (1980) *Surviving The Break-Up: How Children Cope With Divorce.* London: Grant McIntyre Ltd.

Wallerstein, J. and Blakeslee, S. (1990) *Second Chances.* London: Corgi.

Ward, B. (1995) *Good Grief 1*. London: Jessica Kingsley.

Wicks, B. (1988) *No Time To Wave Good-Bye*. London: Bloomsbury.

Wollington, T. (1988) *I'm Still Running*. Pub. by St. Luke's Hospice and CLIC (Cancer and Leukaemia in Childhood Trust.)

Worden, J.W. (1983) *Grief Counselling and Grief Therapy*. London: Tavistock.

Zeman, S. (1997) 'A Keen Eye For Danger', report in *The Guardian*, July 15th.

Index